External Challenges to Management Decisions: A Growing International Business Problem

Report No. 808

The Conference Board

ABOUT THE CONFERENCE BOARD

The Conference Board is an independent, not-for-profit research institution with facilities in the United States, Canada and Europe. Its scientific studies of management and economics produce a continuing flow of timely and practical information to assist leaders of business, government, labor and other institutions in arriving at sound decisions. The Board's research is also made available to the news media in order to contribute to public understanding of economic and management issues in market economies.

Worldwide, The Conference Board is supported financially by more than 4,000 Associates, comprised of corporations, national and regional governments, labor unions, universities, associations, public libraries and individuals.

THE BOARD'S SERVICES

Research reports, personalized information services and access to a variety of meetings are among the direct benefits that Associates receive from The Conference Board. Associate Relations representatives at the address listed below will describe these activities in detail and will tailor delivery of Board services to the specific needs of Associate organizations. Inquiries from locations other than in Canada and Europe should be addressed to The Conference Board, Inc. in New York.

The Conference Board, Inc.
845 Third Avenue, New York, New York 10022
(212) 759-0900
Telex: 234465 and 237282

The Conference Board in Canada
Suite 100, 25 McArthur Road, Ottawa, Ontario K1L-6R3
(613) 746-1261

The Conference Board in Europe
Avenue Louise, 207 - Bte 5, B-1050 Brussels, Belgium
(02) 640 62 40
Telex: 63635

Conference Board Report No. 808   Printed in U.S.A.

ISBN No.:0-8237-0244-8

Cover Design by Jimi M. Patricola

External Challenges to Management Decisions:

A Growing International Business Problem

by Allen R. Janger
Director, Management Research
and
Ronald E. Berenbeim
Senior Research Associate

A Research Report from The Conference Board

Contents

Tables

Authors' Acknowledgments

The authors wish to thank several persons and organizations for valuable assistance at various stages of this project. Vladimir Pucik conducted many of the interviews and assisted with the arrangements for the Japanese portion of the study. His facility with the Japanese language and his knowledge of Japanese business culture proved invaluable. In Europe, Christopher Carnaghan, then of The Conference Board in Europe, conducted a number of interviews and added insights to the analysis.

Other individuals and groups were especially helpful in arranging interview schedules which made it possible for us to see large numbers of people in a limited period of time. Those individuals and organizations are: Salvador F. Zuniga in Mexico; Eduardo J. Cassullo, Executive Director of IDEA in Argentina; Keith S. Bush and David Reeves in Brazil; and in Japan—Masaya Miyoshi, Managing Director, Keidanran; Naomitsu Yamanouchi, Director—Department for International Affairs, Japan Institute for Social and Economic Affairs; and Tadashi Yamamoto, Director, Japan Center for International Exchange. Finally, Hisao Kanamori, President of the Japan Economic Research Center, extended the hospitality of his organization to the writer of the Japanese chapter in providing him with office space and clerical assistance.

Allen R. Janger
Ronald E. Berenbeim

Foreword

THE WORLD'S senior business executives are finding it increasingly necessary to respond effectively to groups and individuals who are outside the management group, but have their own ideas about how and for what purposes the company should be managed.

The rise of vocal protests has created a decision-making environment with special problems and discomforts for top managers. First, top managers tend to see themselves as "men of responsibility" who make decisions and initiate the events that make things happen in the corporation. They feel threatened by outside challenges to their judgment and authority to make decisions. As a result, these managers are often unwilling to concede that the concern of outsiders with corporate activities may be legitimate. In this atmosphere executives often find it difficult to assess objectively the degree to which these external positions should be—or already have been—incorporated in company decision processes.

Problem two lies—paradoxically—in the relative infrequency of "incidents." Protest groups do not appear at company offices very often and there is a human tendency to regard infrequent and possibly distant occurrences as unimportant, even though the character of the risks they pose may be considerable. For although many business leaders contend that the protest phenomenon started as little more than a left-wing irritation, it now embraces the entire spectrum of political opinion, and all areas of business decision making.

Third, those who have been involved in protest incidents often find it difficult to describe and make credible to other executives their concerns about protest groups. Yet this communication is necessary if protests are to be resolved without running the risk of deep damage to the company.

It is in this context of a changing and problematic decision-making environment that the organizers of the Sixth International Industrial Conference asked The Conference Board to conduct a worldwide study of the impact of outsider activity on company decision making and to examine company responses to these outside challenges.

We gratefully acknowledge the IIC's financial support and the important contribution of time and thought by the senior executives from around the world whose responses to questionnaires and in formal interviews comprise the bulk of data analyzed for this report. A major contribution was made to the design of the research by The Conference Board's Public Affairs Research Council.

KENNETH A. RANDALL
President

Chapter 1
The External Challenge and the Company Response—
An International Overview

As THE DECADE of the 1980's begins, business institutions around the world, in the eyes of their senior executives, face a growing challenge to their companies' continued freedom of action. This challenge, which knows no geographical or political boundaries, can be found to a greater or lesser degree in all kinds of economic and political systems. The challenge is in the form of a demand by people outside management for participation—in the name of the larger public good—in decisions traditionally reserved to management, such as hiring policy and plant location.

This challenge comes primarily in the form of government-sponsored regulation and economic planning, but in many areas of the world the challenge also comes from ordinary citizens, from organized and semi-organized social and political groups, and from unions and religious groups seeking objectives and utilizing methods unfamiliar to many of their members.

The visual image of this larger, nongovernmental challenge is the "incident of protest" in which outsiders appear at the gates of a company facility armed with signs and leaflets to protest some company decision or to object to some aspect of the company's conduct. The protesting group has usually made some effort to make its demands known to the media and the press is often in attendance.

It is this demand for recognition by a citizenry, acting in the name of the "public interest," and utilizing the format and tactics of "political protest" that leads executives to describe the phenomenon as primarily political in nature, and sometimes to refer to the current era as one in which the corporation has been "politicized." Of course, this "politicization" does not stop with demonstrations at the plant gates, but involves a whole range of methods and devices appropriate to the political arena—media events, legislative lobbying, confrontation, negotiation and litigation.

In this new environment, social and political dimensions have been added to the traditional business planning of the company, and new actors have been added to the cast of characters having a more or less direct impact on the company's decision-making process. Executives are noticeably reticent about characterizing these changes. Contemporary trends in the corporate etiquette of most countries require that, wherever possible, changes in levels of authority and requirements for further consultation be muted for the sake of corporate harmony. The trend toward a more participative management process is also a worldwide phenomenon and the manner in which corporate managements have responded to this kind of stress is, in large measure, the subject of this study. Despite the reluctance to engage in these kinds of discussions, business executives have described several major changes:

(1) Unlike the approach employed in the past, in which the executive "took" a stand that became, in effect, the law of the company, the new environment is one in which decisions are arrived at circuitously, if at all, through negotiations between responsible representatives of the opposing group or groups. In many instances it is deemed appropriate to wait until a certain level of confrontation has been reached in order to identify the leadership and the relative strengths and weaknesses of the challengers.

(2) There may be no "decision" at the end of the process, or at least none in the sense of a clear-cut statement in writing of what all the parties have agreed to do. Out of political confrontations may come nothing more than an informal meeting of the minds, from which the leaders of confronting groups may guide their own internal decisions. Often this vagueness may serve some ultimate purpose by not tying the hands of either party. Another reason why negotiations with pressure groups frequently do not culminate in finding agreements is that

the leaders of these organizations often do not have the authority to commit their members to an agreement. As one executive put it: "If Ralph Nader comes to an agreement with you, what have you got? He may or may not be able to speak for others. In the end he can only agree to stop attacking you."

(3) When outside groups are involved, the decision-making process focuses less on problem solving than on resolution of conflicting values. Traditional business decision making focuses on problem solving within a largely established corporate value system that is shared by all parties. It proceeds by the interaction of people who have relevant knowledge with those who bear responsibility for the solution of the problem. The focus of the discussion is on logic and technical matters. This approach is more difficult in a politicized environment. Because of differences in values, philosophies and conflicting independent interests, decisions resist "scientific," or even rational, analysis. Knowledge and technical judgment may be useful but are not essential, and the people involved may actually know little about the technical aspects of the question. They may have little or no responsibility for implementation of the decision. It was the German philosopher, Kant, who pointed out that logic begins only after questions of value are resolved. Accordingly, over questions of value, power—not logic—rules supreme.

(4) Protests do not follow the chain of command. Typically, protestors seek the nearest company facility for their protest, or choose a site that will make the protest most visible to the media. Rarely do groups carry their protest directly to the staff unit most responsible for studying the issue or to an executive with sufficient and appropriate authority for dealing with it. Yet the early handling of a protest by the first company executives to encounter the protestors can often spell the difference between a protest that dissipates and one that lingers. Early mishandling of a protest can commit the company to undesirable actions and foreclose more favorable ones.

Business executives often complain that once business decisions get into the political sphere they can become difficult and costly to resolve. And, always lurking in the background, is the possibility of the ruinous political issue that can destroy a business.

But evidently it is not these differences alone that concern senior executives. Operating in a "political" environment of the kind described above is not altogether novel to the world's businesses. From the early days of big business, any company that wanted to extract oil or minerals, sell major power or communications systems, or, indeed, sell any major item in a country other than its own, necessarily entered into the political arena in some way. Similarly, the ways in which companies produced and sold their goods, operated their facilities, and treated their employees have been a matter of public debate and political struggle since business's earliest days.

What, then, is different enough about the current environment to lead some executives to refer to a "politicization of the enterprise?" Does it really spell the "end of the free enterprise system as we have known it," as some executives claim? Is it just the latest example of "senior executive whining," as other executives see it? Or does it signify something in between—as implied by the response of one French executive: "I don't know whether free enterprise will end by 1990, but I do know that for business and the business class there will be life after death no matter what happens."

In the interest of finding out exactly what the world's businessmen mean when they talk about the "politicization" of the business atmosphere, what the significance of this change is, and, ultimately what issues this raises for the way in which the enterprise is managed, The Conference Board surveyed executives from some 300 companies by mail questionnaire, and interviewed close to 200 executives. The mail survey included executives from all parts of the world, with strongest emphasis on the industrialized nations and somewhat less on the developing and underdeveloped nations. Although several executives from the Communist world were also surveyed, their views do not form a definable element in the research. This was followed by interviews with executives in 13 countries: the United States, Japan, the United Kingdom, France, Germany, Belgium, the Netherlands, Sweden, Switzerland, Italy, Argentina, Brazil, Chile and Mexico.

The mail questionnaire was designed to throw light on the prevalence of "outside influences" on decision making, the identity and interest of these "outsiders," and the company responses to the presence and demands of outside groups. The interviews were directed at learning more about specific incidents where outsiders had attempted to influence the decision-making process. Executives were asked to identify and describe incidents that had occurred to their companies, and to explore with the interviewer the character and tactics of the company response—and the impact of the experience on their organizations.

Analyzing these responses and data suggest general conclusions relative to the questions posed earlier: (1) the basic character of this new political challenge; (2) the character of the company response; and (3) issues raised for the management of the business.

These issues are explored in general in this chapter. Succeeding chapters will focus on specific countries or areas of the world—the United States, Europe, Japan and Latin America.

The Political Challenge—An Overview

One clearly novel development in the current environment is the increasing volume of political challenge. Some 90 percent of the executives surveyed reported that attempts by nongovernmental "outsiders" to participate

Table 1: Judgments as to whether Outsiders Are Trying to Have an Increasing Influence on or Involvement in Company Decision Making

	All Executives*		United States		Europe		Developing Nations	
	Number	Percent	Number	Percent	Number	Percent	Number	Percent
	210	100%	71	100%	50	100%	58	100%
Yes	195	93	68	96	49	98	48	84
No	15	7	3	4	1	2	10	16

*Includes executives from all parts of the world as well as those from the United States, Europe and the Developing Nations.

in their companies' decision making had increased over the past five years. A major, and perhaps surprising, finding is that *this phenomenon is worldwide in scope.* (Table 1.) Business executives outside the United States, Europe and Japan were slightly less likely to report outside interference (84 percent) than were those from these areas (96 percent or more).

These outsiders do not regard any aspect of company operation as sacrosanct or proprietary. The decision-making areas in which outsiders have tried to participate (see Table 2) cover virtually every aspect of company operation according to business executives.

This is a considerable change from the days when the operations of a firm were largely a closed book to anyone but the managers. Even government regulatory practice has generally been satisfied with proscribing certain kinds of business conduct, apart from which management was free to manage as it saw fit, and was largely free from scrutiny. Even with the passage of the newer equal employment opportunity laws in the United States that seek to encourage social change, managements—through the affirmative action planning process—are made largely responsible for deciding how these social changes will be pursued inside the company.

What is new, in other words, is that increasingly there are outsiders who are not satisfied to allow managers to manage the firm as they see fit.

• Some do not trust the managers.
• Some do not agree with the economic objectives set by management and would like to replace them with others.
• Some wish to add or give priority to noneconomic objectives.
• Some have special economic or social interests that they want emphasized in the decision-making process.
• Some simply feel that "business is too important for businessmen," and that nonmanagers and nonowners should participate in business decision making.

Further, there are increasingly citizens—among whom must be numbered executives and employees of the companies themselves—who are not satisfied to pursue social change by having governments pass and enforce laws. Rather, they wish actually to participate in the

enactment, and aid in the fulfillment of plans and the planning processes.

Sources of Outside Pressure

A major new source of outsider pressure has been a host of what are sometimes referred to as "single interest" or "single issue" groups, so-called because of the relative narrowness of their interests. Typically, they represent the interests of a single social group, or they may focus on a single or closely related set of issues.

The most active during the period under study were:

Environmental groups, such as the "Sierra Club" in the United States and the "Friends of the Earth" in various countries of Europe. These groups have been among the most active of single-interest groups worldwide; some 56 percent of the responding companies reported some form of confrontational contact with these groups, (see Table 3 on page 5).

Consumer groups, such as the various groups organized under the sponsorship of Ralph Nader in the United States and the so-called "Housewives Associations" in Japan. About 43 percent of the companies reported conflicts with these groups.

Racial minority and ethnic groups pressured some 35 percent of the managements, most often for increased job opportunities for the members of the minority or ethnic groups they represent or to support political positions.

Ad hoc community groups were cited as a source of outside pressure by about one-third (32 percent) of the companies. Such groups were usually made up of local residents who organized to deal with very specific local problems: the development of a piece of real estate as, for example, the real-estate development explored in Chapter 2; or conditions in the environment around a plant, as described in Chapter 3.

Women's and feminist groups had contacted just over one-fifth (22%) of the companies. they were mainly interested in such issues as hiring and social welfare policies, pay, and the like as they bore on women in the workplace.

Handicapped individuals groups had contacted about 15 percent of the companies. They were interested in

Table 2: Kinds of Decisions in which Outsiders Try to Participate

In What Kinds of Decisions Did They Try to Participate?	Worldwide*		United States		Europe		Developing Nations	
	Companies	Percent	Companies	Percent	Companies	Percent	Companies	Percent
	214	100%	72	100%	50	100%	65	100
Location of Facilities	31	15	10	14	8	16	9	14
Financial and Investment Policies...............	24	11	7	10	10	20	5	8
Expansion and Reduction of Facilities............	23	11	7	10	5	10	5	8
Pay and Social Welfare Practices..............	23	11	5	7	7	14	10	15
Hiring Practices..........	19	9	10	14	4	8	4	6
Advertising and Pricing....	17	8	4	6	6	12	5	8
Layoff and Redundancy ...	16	8	3	4	4	8	4	6
Product Design, Function, Use	15	8	4	6	4	8	4	6
Purchasing Processes	12	6	5	7	1	2	4	6
Production Processes.....	8	4	1	1	2	4	4	6
New Product Research	5	2	2	3	1	2	2	3

*Includes companies from all parts of the world as well as those from the United States, Europe and the Developing Nations.

employment, compensation, training and advancement of handicapped individuals.

Such groups, emerging from the political ferment of the 1960's, and reflecting the issue-oriented militancy of the time, tend to be uppermost in the minds of executives when they talk about outsider influence. But these groups are not the only new sources of outsider group pressure, nor even the most active. For in the new environment many companies, for example, have experienced pressure from groups that are not usually thought of in connection with confrontation politics:

Trade unions were cited as having attempted to participate in business decision making in seven out of ten (71 percent) of the companies. These were mainly over such issues as plant closings, plant staffing levels, and the like. But Swedish unions have been active in a wide range of social issues, for example, pressing a number of Swedish employers to encourage black unions in their facilities in South Africa. In France, also, a number of trade unions made an attempt to press employers on consumer protection matters.

Political parties attempted to shape company decisions among more than half the companies surveyed (47 percent). They rarely were initiators of issues, however, usually intervening—or being brought in—only after confrontations had already developed.

Business and industry groups had been involved with about 40 percent of the companies, pressing for company support for business and industry positions, or for participation in social programs sponsored or conducted by the group. Energy policy—and especially support for some use of nuclear power—has been a prime area of business militancy. A special case is Latin America, where business and industry associations have always played an important role in decision making. Although they continue to play an important role, there is little evidence to date that the industry associations have attempted to influence the policies of individual companies as they relate to social or political issues.

Religious groups had contacted about 35 percent of the companies on a wide variety of issues. The main activists have been the Catholic Church and the various arms of the World Council of Churches. Issues in which they have been active: (1) South African investment, (2) baby food advertising and promotion practices in Africa, and (3) the welfare of the poor in some countries in Latin America. The distinguishing characteristic of most church groups is that they pursue issues on behalf of the dispossessed members of society and do not stand to gain from the outcome.

U.S. companies feel that pressure groups are more active in their country than elsewhere. In the United States, the average responding company had been contacted by no fewer than five different types of outside pressure groups. Moreover, the more narrowly focused single-interest groups have tended to predominate in the United States, with the most active groups working in relatively specific areas of environmental, minority-ethnic, and religious concern.

While pressure groups have been quite active in Sweden and the Netherlands, the average European management has had fewer types of groups to contend with. This is due in many instances to the greater homogeneity of their populations. Still more to the point, the external challenges have been funneled through and articulated by the more broadly focused political parties

Table 3: Outsiders Attempting to Participate in Company's Decision Making

What Groups Have Attempted to Participate in Your Company's Decision Making?	Worldwide*		United States		Europe		Developing Nations	
	Companies	Percent	Companies	Percent	Companies	Percent	Companies	Percent
	214	100%	72	100%	50	100%	65	100
Unions..................	151	71	40	56	41	82	42	65
Environmental Groups	119	56	49	68	27	54	23	35
Political Parties	100	47	19	26	31	62	30	46
Consumers Groups	91	43	33	46	22	44	21	32
Business and Industry Associations	85	40	23	32	20	40	31	48
Minority and Ethnic Groups	74	35	49	68	8	16	8	12
Religious Groups.........	74	35	44	61	12	24	10	15
Community Groups	69	32	36	50	12	24	12	18
Women's and Feminist Groups	46	22	29	40	6	12	5	8
Handicapped Individuals ..	32	15	16	22	5	10	4	6
Others.................	40	19	9	13	12	24	15	23

*Includes companies from all parts of the world as well as those from the United States, Europe and the Developing Nations.

and trade unions, rather than by single interest groups, and are expressed as part of the "big" issues of worker democracy and codetermination.

In the countries of Latin America, nongovernmental pressure groups have tended to be considerably less active, the majority of the responding managements having only the unions and, in some cases, the Catholic Church, to deal with. Business and industry groups and government have been far more active than any of the newer style social groups. Indeed, looking at the past five years, only environmental and consumer groups are significantly mentioned by the surveyed companies.

Japan has fewer examples of protest, but some of the incidents that have arisen have an unusual ferocity by Western standards. For Japan has especially active pressure groups in environmental and consumer areas; more active, indeed, than anywhere outside the United States.

A characteristic feature of many of these newer interest groups is their international, or at least supranational, perspective. Internationalism has always been a claim of the trade union movement, of course, but among the newer trade union pressure groups, the International Metal Workers and the International Chemical Workers have taken as one of their aspirations the development of collective bargaining across national lines. Much more to the point, a number of the issues raised by the groups, such as a number of campaigns aimed at South African racial problems, or the promotion and marketing of baby formulas in Africa, are designed to bring pressure in localities many borders distant from the countries most directly affected.

Corporate executives claim, too, that a kind of international network supports and, to some degree,

coordinates the work of pressure groups. Anti-nuclear power groups over the entire world are said to utilize research information, expertise and experts developed in other countries, especially in the United States and Sweden. Local environmental and community groups, fighting plans to set up oil-producing facilities along the Scottish coast, brought in experts from the Massachusetts Institute of Technology to testify at local hearings. International funding and support of pressure groups in Latin America and Africa are publicly acknowledged by the Social Democratic parties of Germany and Sweden. Private foundation support has also crossed national lines.

What Are Their Tactics?

Confrontation is the weapon of the outside interest group, the most notorious example of which is the political demonstration, the "incident of protest" cited at the beginning of this chapter. In the strictest sense of the word, these kinds of incidents are theater—for they concentrate on the drama of a given situation rather than on its substance. This reliance on an appeal to emotions by a skillful manipulation of the dramatic force inherent in the confrontation between a small and powerless group doing battle with a large organization over issues of justice and social responsibility guarantees a large audience through widespread media coverage.

These tactics are designed to overcome the fact that these groups often lack traditional grounds for getting management to pay attention to them. Unions may be able to make a claim to discuss plant relocation decisions, but when they join with religious organizations to demand changes in investment policy or in product design their negotiating status is more questionable. Less well-known groups may give rise to doubts by executives as to who—if anyone, besides themselves—the group's leaders represent.

Saul Alinsky, who trained agitators in the early 1960's, called such demonstrations the "tactics of weakness." They are the adult equivalent of a child's tantrum. They are most effective when practiced by the young or by people with little socioeconomic status or power. They dramatize the outsiders' ability to disrupt and disorganize. They trade on the protestors' sense of grievance and on the public's sense of guilt as means to make those they wish to influence tolerate their "outrageous conduct."

But what happens after the demonstrators have gained managerial attention? Clearly outsider tactics only begin with the protest demonstration. And there are, of course, other protestors who would never think to use a demonstration either to gain the corporate attention or to gain the desired change in decision—but they, too, have never lacked for tactical weapons. Other available tactical approaches are:

• *Persuasion and negotiation,* in which the protestors attempt to get the management to agree with the protestors' point of view. Facts and arguments are presented. The logic and desirability of the protestors' demands are emphasized. This tactic is most often pursued where the protestors believe no sharp conflict exists between the values of the protestors and management. Management is believed to lack the relevant facts, or not to have considered all relevant issues.

• *Legal and judicial,* in which the protestors use the laws, the courts, and the broader framework of administrative hearings and orders to further their objectives. Criminal and civil suits may be instituted. Injunctions may be sought to enjoin company action. These tactics are usually most actively pursued where the protestors do not believe that management is open to persuasion, and that only an adversary approach will force management to modify its objectives. In administrative hearings the workings of the law create an adversary environment which protestors may use to further their objectives.

• *Market forces,* in which the protestors use an array of weapons designed to weaken the company's economic position, and thereby force the management to agree to the protestors' demands. Strikes and boycotts may be conducted against the company's products.

• *Investment position,* in which the protestors use an investor or ownership position in a company to change or modify management and to set objectives. The most common tactic is the stockholder resolution.

• *Media,* in which print and the electronic media are used as vehicles for airing the protestors' perspective and to gain legitimacy for their objectives before a wider

public. The tactic is designed to influence public opinion—and, in some cases, political parties—in order to bring pressure to bear on management.

What about physical violence? Clearly there are areas of the world where the threat or actual use of violence—sabotage, assaults, kidnappings, assassinations and the like—are habitually used by outsiders to force managers to do their will. Also there are more or less "peaceable" demonstrations that become violent. But, by and large, the tactics of outsiders are nonviolent, and the protestors usually see the demonstration itself as an alternative to violence. "In the tactics of protest," one group leader explained, "we seek for means to struggle with companies without actually fighting."

No matter which tactic is used, the main protagonists of the action are the protestors and management. Except for incidents in which persuasion, negotiation or violence are the exclusive tactics, there may be other protagonists as well. In some instances, notably when the courts are brought into the picture, these outsiders may so overwhelm the process that the main protagonists may effectively lose control of the outcome.

In major protests and confrontations more than one tactical approach is often utilized. Persuasion and negotiation may be used at various phases of a confrontation and in coordination with moves in the courts and in the press. Persuasion and negotiation tactics are said to predominate where there is general agreement on values. Adversary tactics involving the courts, administrative hearings, and the press are less frequent, but generally arise where negotiation is not likely to produce a desirable outcome from the protestors' point of view. Violence is most often employed where established institutions do not provide an adequate forum for the airing of grievances.

The complexity of modern social and economic organization often makes it easier, rather than harder, for a single-minded protest group to obstruct business activity. A British executive observed: "This puts the protestor in the situation of the Roman soldier, Horatius, who could single-handedly obstruct an entire enemy army because the army had to cross a river at a narrow bridge before it could go on about its business. Our complex economy is filled with 'narrow bridges' and a determined minority can effectively prevent action, even desirable action, and be considered as heroes for it."

The Company Response

Feelings...

The style of protest is often provocative and repellent. But it is not just the style of outside protest that rubs executives the wrong way. Ultimately, even executives who might otherwise be sympathetic to the views of the outside groups are irritated at having people looking over their shoulders. Few, if any, executives really like to be second-guessed. This very human trait is a major source of staff-line and intraorganizational conflict. The level of executive resentment may be even greater if that interference comes from outside the company.

Other executives object to outside protest as an illegitimate invasion of management prerogatives. As one American executive put it, in a classic statement of the position: "They have no right to ask us to do anything. They are not the owners; they do not represent the owners. They are elected by nobody and represent no one but themselves."

Still other executives see outside protestors as a counterproductive force: "They muddy the waters of decision with foolish arguments and unrealistic objectives." A Swedish executive ridiculed the attempts of environmentalists to get a "risk-free" environment "in a world where assuming one risk is the price of minimizing another." This, of course, shows the difference in perspective between business and many environmental groups.

As one British executive put it: "We are interested in 'managed risk'—the trade-off between risks and benefits. Homeowners are not interested in this kind of equation, they want perfect safety." Executives feel that protest ups the price and makes it harder for business to act in a careful and responsible manner. A German executive said: "They encourage irresponsible behavior, in us as well as in themselves." A quarter of the responding executives are convinced that such groups do not even make a constructive contribution. They agreed with the survey statement: "All valid social and economic changes would occur in our company without outsider activity." Almost one-third (31 percent) credited outsider groups with making "valid social and economic changes occur that would not otherwise occur." Almost half (44 percent) rejected both statements, possibly because, as one executive put it: "There are benefits, but they are not worth the costs."

...And Judgments

Still, whatever their emotions, convictions or reservations, the vast majority of managers, when faced with protests from outside, feel they must sit down and at least talk with the protestors. Only a handful (under 1 percent) of the responding executives said they "resisted all attempts at direct communication."

Most executives find the majority of intrusions so minor and so reasonable that they would not resent or reject them out of hand. There is even the possibility that the criticism may be helpful. As one American executive put it: "Who can get excited when a local community group reminds you of something your executives should have thought of in the first place?" However, the company's view as to the reasonableness of the request is

hardly ever the sole test for a group's impact in decision making.

As executives see it, these outsider groups tend to get much of their leverage because it is felt that they are able to influence government decisions and actions (81 percent), or would supply future leadership to political parties and administrative agencies (33 percent in the United States and Europe and 20 percent in other countries). One of the major reasons cited by executives for responding to outsider demonstration and protests was the possibility that, if not properly handled, the result would be restrictive legislation. The consensus view is that: "It is better to deal with individual and group grievances and to respond to their demands within the framework of a company or industry association than to risk government or political party involvement that will result in the rigidities of legislative regulation."

Nor is that the only result of badly handled protest incidents. Companies worry that getting a reputation for being "hard-nosed," "unresponsive," or "socially irresponsible," will lead to difficulties in hiring top-flight technical and scientific personnel, will adversely affect the price of their equities, and will lead to more difficult and expensive bank financing.

Whom Companies Respond To

Outsiders gain legitimacy for their assaults on the corporate decision-making process by asserting a role as advocates of cultural and human values allegedly ignored by the corporation, or left unprotected by the normal actions of companies and government. Their tactics arise from the complex interrelated nature of modern society and economic operations. As a result of the need to integrate activities in order to protect one part of the society and economy from unanticipated damage that might result from decisions in the other parts, there are many safety levers for obstructing action to those who know where they are and how to use them—the courts, administrative hearings, the communications media, and the political parties.

Companies do not treat all protestors in the same way, nor do they give all protestors equal attention. Those protestors get most attention, and even deference, who:

(1) *know how to accumulate and deploy political power with confrontational sophistication.* The possession by groups and their supporters of money, influence, access to high political or governmental officials, large membership, powerful allies, and skilled leadership is a clear consideration in determining how fully and how companies will deal with outside pressure groups.

How well do the protestors utilize the media? Notice in the media confers legitimacy on the grievances, and upon the organization that advances them. This forces the company involved to take a protest group seriously. Lack of press attention often identifies a cause that companies can safely ignore.

(2) *understand the importance of making and keeping agreements.* Protestors who "play the game, and play it straight" get more attention than those who cannot do so—or who choose not to.

The protestors' "sincerity" was a consideration that cropped up in almost every company and every country. In Japan, for example, they refer to the seriousness with which the protestors conduct the grievance protest. In the United States, "sincere" protestors are those who seem truly interested in the problem, who wish to learn more about it, and who are anxious to resolve it in a practicable way. "Sincere" in the United States is largely synonymous with "reasonable" and "good faith." In the minds of many European executives the issue of sincerity is usually linked with whether the protestors are felt to be using the issue unduly to build the strength of the protesting organization.

No matter what the country, in any protest situation executives find themselves making judgments about the protestors' sense of proportion, their interest in the subject, their openness to compromise, and their hidden or secondary objectives. All of these considerations come into play in deciding how seriously to treat a given protest, and how much recognition to give a protesting organization. Higher levels of education have produced increasing numbers of the kinds of people who not only know where the levers are, but who feel no compunction at pulling them if their values or interests are threatened.

The power of such outsider groups has grown to the point where almost half the executives (47 percent) worldwide felt that "on selected issues" outsiders have more influence than government. Those questioned believe that outsider group power is stronger in the United States and Europe, where almost six out of ten (57 percent) of the executives felt that protest organizations had exerted more influence than government on some company issues. Outsider group power is regarded as considerably weaker in Latin America. Most executives felt that government was always more influential (60 percent) than outsider groups, especially in Latin America (73 percent).

Indeed, in a recent Conference Board survey, chief executives of U.S. firms, when asked to name the most influential members of U.S. life, included two outsider leaders, Ralph Nader and John Gardner. Ralph Nader, in fact, was named by almost half (49 percent) of the responding executives—more than anyone except the then trade union leader, George Meany—and well ahead of any business executive.[1]

[1]P. Bonfield, *"U.S. Business Leaders: A Survey of Opinions and Characteristics.* The Conference Board, Report No. 786, 1980.

Because of their influence, many executives feel they must respond to protest incidents by dealing directly with the protestors. These dealings are characterized in a number of different ways, which reflect differences in handling the confrontation experience. However, none of the dealings necessarily lessen the fundamentally adversarial character of the confrontation.

How Companies Respond

In describing their responses to incidents, the largest number of companies (40 percent) characterized them primarily as exchanges of views. "We will receive outsiders' views and will communicate our own to them," was the phrase they selected from the questionnaire. Most of those who described their dealings with outsiders as primarily an exchange of views saw such meetings as only one stage—and usually a preliminary stage at that—in a longer adversary relationship. "We got our views out on the table at these early discussions," is how one U.S. executive described a struggle with an environmental group. "We did not agree on much and we knew the real confrontation would be in the courts." The exchange may have less to do with a real communication of views than with taking the measure of opposition groups and developing a feel for the nature and quality of their positions and leadership.

A second, almost equally numerous, group of companies (38 percent) go beyond mere exchange of viewpoints or position to attempt to clarify the issues. They said they "will discuss views with outsiders to clarify facts about the issues." Generally speaking, the companies that recount their approach in these terms have had fewer, or at least less critical, confrontations. The confrontations they have had seem to result in the opportunity for conciliation. For them "clarification of the issue" has evidently carried a strong possibility of resolving issues without extensive delays or recourse to the courts.

There is also a group of companies (14 percent) to whom confrontation amounts to "persuasion." They characterize their confrontational stance in terms such as: "We will discuss opinions with outsiders with a view to persuading them of the rightness of our position." Many of these companies are large, multinational corporations with one or two major issues that are critical to their existence—for example, the major nuclear power suppliers; or potentially embarrassing to their senior managements—as in the case of a multinational bank's investment in South African business.

Finally, a few (4 percent) of the companies see their discussions as aimed toward "collaborative accommodation." They describe their stance in such terms as "will discuss views with outsiders with a view to compromise."

Collaborative approaches may lead to joint projects in

which both companies and protestors take leadership. Polaroid, the U.S. camera manufacturer, for example, joined with a protest group of employees to improve the racial conditions in the company's South African subsidiary. Several Swedish companies did the same through collaborative action with the Swedish labor movement. Philips explored plant-closing procedures with its unions. Such collaborative efforts generally reflect a broad commonality of interest, a significant opportunity for the company to improve conditions or gain objectives which may be distantly related to the protest incident, and deep trust between company and protest-group leadership.

These examples also entail a certain amount of risk—Philips' local unions ultimately attempted to expand the collaborative effort to overseas operations, which the company resisted. Still, collaborative efforts can be very successful for all participants. Philips' collaborative effort with a Marxist filmmaker (described in the European chapter) is a case in point. And the memories of such successes tend to tower in the memories of executives.

None of the approaches (exchange of views, clarification of issues, persuasive or collaborative accommodation) can be said to be characteristic of dealings in any one part of the world, or of any one type of company. As already implied, collaborative approaches were noted among manufacturing as well as non-manufacturing U.S. and European companies. Companies in "controversial" businesses (which can include businesses as different as baby food, petroleum and power generation) are more likely to feel the need to take "persuasive" approaches.

Differences in Approach

How do these differences in approach manifest themselves? In general, the U.S. executives tended to see individual protests as part of a larger and more formal process, while the Europeans and the Japanese usually took a more informal approach. In the mail survey, for example, most U.S. executives (54 percent) described their approach in the "exchange of views" terminology.

The European executives, in contrast, most frequently (40 percent) characterized their companies' approach in the "clarification of views" terminology. Moreover, during interviews with The Conference Board, the European and Japanese executives were far more likely to understand the conflict from the perspective of the protestors than were the Americans. They conceded far more frequently than the Americans the existence of "reasonable aspects" to the protestors' demands. They even, on occasion, were willing to assert a commonality of values and interests with the protestors, something U.S. executives rarely asserted except as a tactical ploy.

Among the Dutch, Swedes, Germans and Japanese, executives seemed to find it fitting to assert a cultural

kinship with the protestors that gives the protestors standing to be heard. Far more European executives, for example, characterized their approaches as "persuasive." "Persuasive" and "two-way clarification" approaches accounted for over three-quarters (76 percent) of the Europeans, but only about two-fifths (39 per cent) of the Americans.

Many executives felt there was a significant difference in approach between the United States and Europe. These contrasts have become the subject of debate and contention between the United States and European segments of multinational corporations. Indeed, they form one aspect of what one French executive referred to as "le mal Americain"—too much individualistic competitiveness, too many lawyers, too much law, too many conflicting interests. A Swedish executive, who recently returned from the United States, observed: "America has the best doctors, the best research people, the best violinists, maybe even the best educated, most energetic executives. But it doesn't seem to be able to get them all together. The devices for integrating U.S. national life have always seemed tumultuous to us, and now they do not seem to be working."

Of course, this competitiveness and the conflicting interests of American life have been productive of great industrial and economic success. The United States may well have evolved to what this individual referred to as an "integrating" phase in its national life. Since the course of American history and the development of its culture have been very different from that of most European countries and Japan, this process of integration may be very difficult for management in the United States.

The critical posture assumed by the European executives relative to the United States reflects a current satisfaction with the way they were handling their own outsider pressures, compared with the experience of the United States. As recently as 1977, though, many Europeans were not nearly so sanguine about their future, and one of the reasons for their pessimism was a "device for integrating their national life": the recent introduction of the industrial democracy laws that put employees on the supervisory boards of directors of many European firms, and which fostered strong, active works councils. The terrorist activities that persisted in Germany and Italy also cast doubt as to whether certain segments of the population could ever be "integrated."

More recently, terrorism has ebbed in Europe, and the industrial developments which European executives feared would undercut managerial authority and prerogatives have turned out to have less fearsome consequences in practice. Indeed, European businessmen have found them to provide more effective devices than previously existed for limiting and defining outsider assaults. Also, they appear in a number of instances to have helped resolve outsider grievances in ways more acceptable to the companies.

Outsider Impact on Decisions: An Assessment

Nor have these differences in approach necessarily led to any substantial loss in management prerogatives. There is a very wide consensus among the world's business leaders that the outsider impact on business decisions has been generally contributory rather than decisive. Only 3 percent of the executives describe outsider impact on their companies' business decisions as "often decisive, leading to acceptance or rejection of a business proposal in many cases." In contrast, nearly half (46 percent) see outsider impact as being only "occasionally decisive, leading to the acceptance or rejection of a business proposal in some cases." An almost equal proportion (45 percent) see the outsiders' impact as utterly contributory, leading at most "to minor modifications in the content of the plan or its timing," but "never decisive." A somewhat larger proportion of the Europeans credited the outsiders with "occasionally decisive" impact on decisions (56 percent) than did U.S. companies (43 percent).

"Politicizing" the Corporation

When executives speak of "politicizing" the corporation they are not speaking merely of how outsiders are attempting to influence the company, nor only about how the corporation responds to each separate incident. They are also speaking of attendant changes in the corporation's policies and management structure. Many speak of "politicizing the corporation" in much the same way that an automobile owner might speak of "winterizing" the car.

Some, who have not been affected by external forces, may see little or no reason to adjust. Others, who have already felt the full blasts of the politicized environment, have made major rearrangements in management policy and structure. But a corporation is also different in important respects from an automobile. There is no owner's manual to tell corporations exactly what to do. Nor can executives simply bring in the mechanics to readjust the corporate mechanism. Shaping the company's relationship to the outside world is a responsibility of the highest authority in the company, and revising that relationship raises issues that are rarely delegated to others.

The vast majority of the companies analyzed faced their first protest incidents without settled policies or procedures for handling such episodes. The "organization structure" for handling the crisis often was the accidental product of where the incident occurred and which executives happened to be on the spot to deal with it. In retrospect, such incidents were often seen as having been dealt with by the wrong person in the organization. With the perspective of hindsight, the settlements were often judged to have been either too conciliatory and accommodating to the outside group—

or too severe. Either way, they were often regarded by executives who had participated in the incidents—or who had thought they should have been involved—as being too limited, or misdirected, or inadequate.

Experience seems to teach executives that a major company cannot get along in the current environment without a planned external relations policy or strategy. Planning policy typically raises a series of difficult issues for top management.

A number of the issues are usually summed up in terms that relate to a series of approaches that have to do with the activity and posture of the company and with the image it wants to project as to responsibility and accountability:

Passive and reactive—in which the company reacts to outsider assaults only after they have been mounted. It defends only where attacked and has no professed public policy objectives. The company draws as little attention to itself as possible and, in effect, attempts to disappear into its surroundings.

Active and anticipatory—in which the company tries to identify outsider assaults before they occur and attempts to head them off. The company has a framework of public policy objectives and values which it seeks to achieve. When pursuing these objectives it acts as a pressure group in the larger society.

Most companies do not fit neatly into either category. As they develop political objectives and strategies they generally tend to move toward the more active-anticipatory end of the spectrum. They formulate public policy objectives, evolve means of anticipating outside challenges and becoming responsive to them, and develop the kind of credible visibility the purpose of which is roughly equivalent to that of the protest groups' demonstrations: The company gets people to listen to what the leadership is saying and to respect what it wants to achieve.

In the past, company external interests tended to be ad hoc and narrowly focused on specific interests and events. Later, as the interests grew in number and complexity, they came to be perceived as interlocking with one another and with the larger social and economic issues affecting the societies in which the company operated. Thus, while many companies continue to deal only with the issues raised by outsiders, and in response to specific situations, top managements increasingly feel they must take a broader approach. Consistent with this development, categories of the company's potential range of interests have developed along the following lines:

Industry scoped: The company feels it must deal in an anticipatory and active manner with public issues generated by changes in technology and political conditions as they bear on the economic conduct of the company. This view can be very narrowly construed, as when a public utility speaks out on the subject of nuclear power plants. Or it may be broadly construed: A bank executive speaking on the subject of nuclear power plants because energy policy is seen as basic to the company's future business plans.

Business scoped: The company feels that it must concern itself with issues relating to the survival of the "business society." Sometimes these issues become the focus of executive attention as in the instance of the U.S. executive, cited earlier in this chapter, who wondered along with many of his confreres whether the current political challenge did not spell the early end of the free enterprise system. More often, the issue hangs a bit in the background, embedded in other issues. For example, during the Swedish nuclear power referendum in the Spring of 1980, Swedish executives raised, among a number of reasons for their choice among alternatives, the fact that the other alternatives would be so economically punishing to power utilities that it would undercut the ability of Swedish businesses to survive.

Society scoped: The company feels it must address issues of what kind of society people should live in. World overpopulation, human rights, and disease prevention in developing countries are usually problems corporate managements leave to governments and to international agencies. But some executives argued that, given the major corporations' economic power and control of technology, governments cannot deal with these problems on their own. "Business and government must find cooperative modes for dealing with these problems which threaten our existence," was the way a German executive phrased it. When utilizing this approach a company may operate as a pressure group, seeking support in the political arena, like other pressure groups, for its views. Or it may involve itself in cooperative projects and ventures with other groups and agencies of government.

Overall, companies are much more likely to take positions on public issues that relate to the company and its industry than on those that relate to business as an institution. They are least likely to involve themselves in issues of how society itself should be organized and managed.

These reasons are often practical. Businessmen express reservations at involving themselves in matters on which they do not believe they have technical knowledge. There is also some question of the legitimacy of professional managers using the resources of the organizations at their command to promote their own social ideas and personal values.

Hence the instincts of many businessmen are to take positions only on matters that are "close to home" both from a technical and an interest point of view. And "social responsibility" usually means participating in programs involving other companies, like the U.S.

National Alliance of Businessmen's JOBS program, where the initiative has come from outside business (in this case, from government).

In general, larger companies take a more broadly based view of their roles than do smaller ones, with social roles often being taken by any companies that play an especially prominent or visible role in the economy of the country. Major multinational corporations almost uniformly take a strong social-responsibility role, but, except in their home countries, carefully avoid taking value-setting roles. Family-owned firms, often take society-focused stands in one or another aspect of their operation. Diversity in business pursuits also seems to affect diversity in political stances. By and large, the more unrelated businesses in which a company engages, the greater the tendency for the company to stay away from global positions and restrict itself to company-specific positions related to specific businesses.

But the issues of scope remain at least somewhat open for most of the executives interviewed. Pragmatically, many of the executives of large companies have concluded that they have little choice but to develop a broader perspective than in the past. Their attitude is partly defensive. Many executives of large companies feel that "tall towers attract attention and lightning." Also, the same desire for active participation that has brought outsiders to feel they must insert themselves into the business-decision process has made executives anxious to extend their own reach. "Business has lost too many battles," is the way one executive described the emotions that led to the foundation of the Business Roundtable.

Managements in all of the countries visited are sensitive to charges of business dominance of the society. The countries vary considerably in the tolerance extended to business in speaking out, or taking sides, on social matters. In places like Japan and Sweden, the role is relatively broad. In the United States, there has been an ebb and flow of business influence—strong in the decade or so following each of the World Wars and much more muted at other times.

In any case, the issue of scope, once it has been resolved (and for most companies this resolution has been an ongoing dynamic process of definition and redefinition) opens an array of issues as to how the objectives are to be pursued.

When companies move into a planned, active, anticipatory stance, they find that they are faced with the same problems as the protest groups in building credibility with the press and public. In building coalitions, companies are involved at every turn in determining whom to cooperate with and support, and how support is to be given. Some of these approaches include:

• *Conferring credibility:* In negotiating with another group, a company gives the group some standing in the community. Concluding an agreement with it gives the group still more standing. Printing stories in annual reports or other company publications about the group or its leadership may also enhance group status (although such statements may alternatively convince the public that the group has "sold out," or been coopted by the company, and its leadership is no longer to be trusted.)

• *Money and resources:* Companies may supply funds, people or the use of company facilities for projects or activities sponsored by protest groups.

• *Adopting the same position:* Companies and protest groups that begin as opponents may end as allies, and very effective allies, when dealing with government or with third parties. This has been the experience, for example, of a number of companies and trade unions in Sweden, Germany and France, where joint positions on various social issues emerged from initial confrontations.

• *Collaborative projects:* As already noted, a small number of the companies (4 percent of the respondents) said they had entered into collaborative projects with outsiders on matters of mutual social concern.

• *Join in permanent association:* Generally, companies join only with other companies in permanent associations to advocate positions on social or political issues. This has been a major feature of the company response to outside pressure. "Business coalitions" and "trade and business associations" at local and national levels have acted as buffers between nonbusiness outsider groups and individual companies. Also these groups have served as agents of broad business involvement in community and national concerns.

At this time, in the vast majority of the companies analyzed, the planning and implementation of this more active and anticipatory external relations stance is the property of a few top managers in the company, and of a corporate or group level public affairs staff. Indeed, the assembling of a public affairs staff from newly created staff components, and the reorientation of preexisting public relations staffs is often the first major step toward political involvement.[2]

Most strategies for achieving greater visibility, for identifying and dealing with major external relations issues, for effective representation of company interests with the major external audiences and outside pressure groups center on the effective workings of a public affairs staff. The purpose of this highly centralized approach has been:

(1) To assure that the company develops and maintains a single, integrated external relations policy toward all its external publics, including nongovernmental outside pressure groups.

(2) To provide expert focus on the company's external relationships, thereby freeing the company's middle managers from a task for which they have neither the time, the training, nor, for the most part, the interest.

In large measure, this public affairs staff does both the planning and the work. It determines the audiences to be reached, how they are to be addressed, prepares the communications (in the form of publications, movies, television presentations, or advertisements), or contracts to have them done outside by professional "communicators." This staff also establishes the mode of dissemination (buys television time, places articles in magazines, etc.) It leaves the bulk of the company's factory managers and executives with a vague, largely representational, "public service" role.

As the cases outlined in succeeding chapters document, the companies are not, for the most part, dissatisfied with results of this approach. But as time goes on, many companies are developing a more decentralized approach—one in which the local managers carry a greater responsibility for dealing with outside constituencies and presumably develop greater competence for dealing with such protests as arise. Among companies whose businesses are decentralized along regional lines (into regional divisions and groups), these regional managers and their staffs become the local focuses of such activity. Among companies organized along product, market or functional subsidiary lines, regional public affairs staffs may be established to help the local managers carry out and coordinate their activities with those of other nearby company managers.[3]

Such approaches, it is felt, do more than facilitate dealing with individual confrontations. They also serve generally to incorporate the needs of the political arena into the company's business decisions and decision making.

This incorporation process often works something like this:

• Identification and assessment of outsider views and positions are made a required part of the business plan, and are reviewed along with the rest of the plan.

• Assessments are made at various stages as to the impact of outsider opposition on the profitability and viability of the business plan.

• Plans to contain, blunt or minimize the effects of outsider opposition are developed consistent with the business plan.

---

[2]For more about how these staffs are organized see Phyllis McGrath, *Managing Corporate External Relations.* The Conference Board, Report No. 679, 1976.

[3]For a more detailed report of how companies are preparing managers for this expanded role see: Seymour Lusterman, *Managerial Competence: The Public Affairs Aspects.* The Conference Board, Report 805, 1981.

• Identification and assessment of outsider issues are independently carried out at the corporate level, and incorporated into the strategic planning process. Corporate public affairs deals with larger public issues.

It should be stressed that the need to be more responsive to outside pressures has not changed the basically economic character of the corporation's objectives. As a Swedish executive described it: "There are more factors in the equation, but the 'X' for which we solve is still profitable operation."

Quite clearly, though, the profitable operation that executives seek now includes:

(1) An ability to deal effectively with direct, company-specific outside challenges by protesters of every description; and

(2) An overall approach that seeks to minimize confrontations both on company-specific and larger public issues likely to have an impact on industry and business.

Chapter 2
The United States of America

As THE DECADE OPENS, the politics of the United States is in an exceptionally fragmented state. The "melting pot" is said to be gone. The traditional dominance of "White, Anglo-Saxon, Protestant" values has been supplanted by a culturally "pluralistic" society in which ethnic, religious and social diversity is proclaimed and encouraged.

The old political alliances built around regional and ethnic coalitions have gone into decline. So have the trade unions. The U.S. Constitution and the legal system, which have never promulgated or protected a single way of life, have in recent years increasingly constituted a framework for leading many different kinds of lives.

Over the past 10 years, the U.S. political landscape has become dotted with small groups, each interested in a single issue or in furthering a relatively narrow interest. But here is the rub. This greater fragmentation comes at a time when the complexities of modern social and economic life require greater cooperation and even integration among diverse segments of society. Achieving this integration among a people who see so much of the national life in terms of competition between individuals and groups is a problem that confounds sociologists and politicians.

Although the United States has something of a consensus on many national objectives, such as the need for clean air and racial equality, there are many other issues—energy, abortion, social welfare, for example—that embody deep divisions among individuals and groups as to how people should live, and how the resources and products of the country are to be produced and distributed. There are fierce divisions over the means to reach even those objectives on which people agree—particularly with respect to the role of government in the process. The American legal system, topped by the Supreme Court of the United States, has become the primary forum within which this battle over "means" is waged.

Alone among American institutions, it retains suf-ficient credibility with most factions to resolve these differences. In answer to the question of how to integrate to meet its new problems and conditions, U.S. society poses an answer largely in terms of new laws, more lawyers, and proliferating legal actions. Increasingly, the site of integration for American life is the court of law, and its integrator is a judge.

Only slightly less important as social and political "glue" is the role played by the media—by television and especially by the press. Increasingly, the media have become a kind of social message center and clearing house. What they flag for special attention is regarded as "important." The media—with special emphasis on the press—become, in effect, arbiters of what is "important" and relevant.

Is this role of arbiter entirely legitimate? Does the existence of such a media role bode well for the future of the American Republic? Does the press fill the arbiter role adequately? These questions have become matters of great and continuing controversy. But it is the mere existence of the controversy—the fact that business executives and legislators can get even more excited over these issues than media people themselves—that underlines the importance of the press as the primary communications link.

The result is what is distinctively American in the business decision-making environment. This environment is characterized by its cultural diversity and by the central roles played by small interest groups, by the press, and, above all by the U.S. legal system. What is distinctively American is the depth of adversary feeling—the degree to which company people feel that outsider claims lack a basic legitimacy, a feeling that outsiders often repay in lack of trust, and "unwillingness to compromise." What is also distinctive is the degree of formality of the proceedings and the often extreme cumbersomeness of the decision process.

The cases that make up the bulk of this chapter fall into one of three major categories of management issues:

(1) *How Companies Deal with Incidents:* The first three cases examine specific incidents, exploring how companies deal with them on an ad hoc and planned basis and how, if at all, these dealings affect the business decision-making process. The cases illustrate the ethnic variety and diversity of U.S. "life-styles" and how this diversity impinges on the business decision-making process. The third case traces a quasi-judicial hearing process that lasted nine years and illustrates the ability of local and parochial interests to dominate the decision process, sometimes to the detriment of larger national, regional or long-term concerns.

(2) *How Companies Develop a Strategic Response:* The fourth and fifth cases also deal with incidents, but take a more extended look at how U.S. companies have evolved a broader, companywide response to the politicized decision-making environment in which they found themselves. In each case the companies attempted to ameliorate the worst effects of the U.S. adversary environment by undertaking ongoing dialogues and coalitions with responsible groups.

(3) *How Companies Act as Pressure Groups:* The last case takes a multicompany perspective, examining one issue—energy—as a means of exploring how U.S. companies have begun to work as participants in forming public opinion on the larger issues affecting business and society.

Dealing with Specific Incidents

The vast majority of protest incidents are relatively minor episodes, which companies seek to keep minor by expeditious and effective handling at as early a stage as possible. A major source of such incidents in the United States in recent years has been the attempts by various ethnic groups to achieve greater status. In this description of one such "minor" encounter, a Chicago bank executive describes in his own words how he dealt with such an incident. The tone of the encounter indicates its deeply adversary nature: The executive does not concede the legitimacy of either the challenge or the challenger. Yet the executive did meet with the outsider, "clarified the facts," and resolved the issue with a minor exercise in "persuasion" that won the debate without necessarily changing any minds.

A U.S. Bank Executive

"A couple of years ago I was visited by a person who purported to represent a group of Polish people—in fact it had a Polish name. I had heard of the guy before—a would-be politician. This fellow liked to go on TV, had been on talk shows, and had been quoted in the newspapers. So I had to spend time with him.

"He said he could look at any name and determine whether or not it was Polish. I asked 'What do you think of the name so-and-so. Is that Polish?' He said no. I

responded: 'That's funny. I guess you didn't notice my secretary's name. She's Polish, that's her name, and it was never altered.' That embarrassed him, and I wasn't trying to embarrass him to any significant degree. First, I wanted to check his responses.

"Then I went on to talk about people in the bank whose positions and ideas represented a change from the way things really were at one time. And I talked about that rather openly, saying: 'Listen, I am in a very distinct minority compared with you, and I know what it is like to come from a working-class neighborhood.'

"So I talked a little bit about myself at that point because he was interested in hearing all that. I wasn't trying to con him; I tried to tell him I understood that Polish people had had to change their names to succeed. So if you look at many of our executives' names you'd have no way of knowing that they were of Polish origin. Some people changed their names because they felt they had to do so. Others were asked to change their names. I told him I didn't like that, and it didn't happen anymore.

"But it did mean that there were many Polish people in our management structure whom he couldn't identify. We went on talking for a couple of hours, and finally agreed that this certainly is a deceptive area. Of course, he never did apologize for the way he rammed his way in. I think he tried to call on the president, the chairman, and somehow got bumped over to me."

To summarize: This outsider did not have a case. His facts were wrong, or at least not credible given the company's counterfacts. The implied threat to carry the grievance to the press and television could not be made credible. Such an outsider becomes "dangerous," or at least "creates problems," in the company view only where the company refuses to talk and the outsider is then able to go the media and give the press not only his allegations, but also his charges that the company refused to face them.

Planning a Plant Expansion

In the emerging business environment, outsider pressure often arises when companies make the extensive plant changes that are increasingly necessary to remain competitive. A case in point is a major U.S. producer of paper and newsprint that found it necessary to expand an existing paper manufacturing plant in the rural Midwest and to add to it a paper-pulping operation.

The decision to expand on the existing site was made basically on economic grounds. Without the expansion and modernization of the plant, and the addition of the pulping operation, the company did not see itself able to compete effectively in emerging international markets.

The implementation of the decision to expand, however, was carried through in different form that it might have been had the decision been made ten years earlier. Noxious smelling pulping operations had already caused outsider protests in a number of places around the world. The company management was especially aware of opposition by local groups in Sweden to paper company operations. These protests had ultimately resulted in what were regarded by industry as expensive and overly strict governmental controls on chemical effluents and air pollution.

Indeed, the decision to locate the plant expansion away from population centers was influenced by a desire to minimize risk of outsider opposition. However, locating the plant in a rural area could not be expected by itself to eliminate risk of outside protests. For, as the U.S. management was aware, the Swedish protests had been aroused against rurally sited plants.

When commencing an effort to locate a plant in a given area, therefore, management felt it had little choice but to "lay it all out" in a "high profile" manner. One of the company's executives with major responsibility in this area explained: "I'd say when we do anything that would involve environmental issues we pretty much lay it out. We know we have to take a high profile and tell them beforehand what we are planning to do. We do not try to hide anything because you know it is highly visible—there are a lot of groups all set to go for a cause, and if you get caught trying to hide something in an environmental area, you will really make yourself a lot of trouble."

The campaign to win the approval of residents had two facets. At the outset, the company vigorously attempted to persuade the local population of its good-faith efforts to build a clean pulp mill and to inform them of the expensive exhaustive efforts it was making to accomplish that objective. Secondly, spokespeople emphasized the jobs and benefits to the community. At all times the company stressed its willingness to discuss the issues with any group. Finally, the company reimbursed individuals for inconvenience or loss arising from the building of the plant.

The second phase of the strategy began once the plant was built and in operation. At that point, the plant became a discrete division of the corporation and a division president was chosen who lived in and was well-known in the community. In addition, a public relations manager was hired who was also familiar to the local community.

At the informational stage, the company reinforced its commitment to a "clean mill" with evidence of its effort to keep abreast of the latest technology. Recalling that point, one executive said: "We told them that we had a group that traveled all over the United States, Canada and Europe. Sweden actually had more advanced technology than the United States, but we used the best of everything that we could find. We spent a lot of extra money doing this, and we told them that, too. I think that we spent $11 million extra on that pulp mill to make it more environmentally palatable."

Still, there were those who did not care how "clean"

the mill was, or how many jobs it would provide. One individual said; "I moved up here because I like living in the wilderness. I like to be able to walk 100 yards out my back door and shoot a deer. And I don't care whether we get new jobs up here or not. That's not why I came up here."

The company tried to smooth over this kind of ruffled feelings by discussion where possible. But sometimes it was necessary to compensate individuals for real or imagined damages. As one executive recalled: "We painted some cars that were damaged by airborne particles. We even bought some steaks for a guy who was cooking on an open grill and claimed that we ruined his steaks." Now that the pulp mill is functioning, the divisional president and public relations officer, both area residents, are assigned to handle any further complaints which may arise.

From these discussions it is apparent that the critical stage of potential external interference with decision making is at the outset of a plant-location decision. Once the necessary approval, or at least forbearance, has been secured, good community relations and a positive image can help to maintain the company's position. As one executive noted: "We get the story out, but as far as selling our product—most of the people who buy paper know that some of it comes from old mills that stink, so I don't think that the fact that we may do a better job has much impact on marketing or recruitment of personnel. In the industry, though, we get plusses for being willing to go out and spend money for the latest technology."

The Limits of Compromise

In the course of the interviews carried out for this research project, executives from other countries often characterized the U.S. business attitude toward outsider pressures as rigidly competitive and so unwilling to recognize a common purpose or common interests with the protestors that only struggle was possible. In the case about to be analyzed, however, the company leadership identified strongly with the environmentalist concerns espoused by local community groups, and was only too ready to collaborate with these groups in carrying through what management regarded as an "environmentally responsible" real-estate development scheme. But true compromise did not occur. The word "compromise" did appear in the judgment handed down after nine years by the local planning authorities. But the amended proposal was not regarded as economically feasible by the real-estate development company and the project has been cancelled for all practical purposes.

The major protagonists were the developers and the local community organization. During the period of conflict, several different sets of real-estate development firms came forward with substantially different proposals to develop a large piece of property on the outskirts of a major West Coast city. For the last six years of the struggle, however, the land was controlled by a major real-estate development company which was, in turn, a division of a large conglomerate. Its plan was to turn the parcel of open land into a large-scale, "environmentally responsible" residential development. Its original plan called for cluster siting of large numbers of apartments and single-family dwellings, while leaving more than half the site for unbuilt wilderness and park.

However, for the existing, relatively sparsely settled community, this was hardly a gain. They had been using the area, in the words of one observer, "as an enormous playground" twice the size of the largest park in the area. It was largely a working-class residential area, and the introduction of larger numbers of better-off people would have dramatically changed the character of their community and impaired their political control of it. As the company saw it: "To them the perfect thing was for somebody else to own it and pay taxes on it, but not to do anything with it. And they've been successful. Here we are, 15 years later, and not one nail has been driven in the area."

The community was joined by "no-growth" environmentalists, most of whom came from well-to-do suburbs, and who were anxious to maintain open spaces in the metropolitan area as well as to preserve certain species of imperiled local fauna and flora. It was also supported by the local governmentally funded legal-aid society. These exist throughout the United States to provide legal help to people who cannot otherwise afford it.[1]

Company executives believed that the community's legal affairs counsel had "orchestrated and organized" the opposition to their plan. Other outside observers judged the community and environmental groups to be working more or less independently, although "keeping in touch with one another."

Supporting the company was the local council of building trades unions and others in the construction trades who were interested in the jobs and business expansion that the residential project would generate. A small group of "growth environmentalists" also supported the company plan as a responsible and creative way of dealing with the "inevitable" need for new housing.

A number of government agencies also played peripheral roles in the proceedings because of the many legal and technical requirements that a project of this size entails. Among the requirements was one pressed suc-

cessfully on the developer—to devote a sizable proportion of the residential units to low-cost housing designed for "poor" people.

The arena for the proceedings was mainly the meetings required by state law for public review of real-estate projects. State law required reviews, for example, before a local review board made up of primarily local residents supported by a professional planning staff of state employees, and a county-level review. Various reviews also took place within each of the incorporated localities in which pieces of the land parcel fell.

Such boards are in theory "arenas of compromise and consensus building." But when polarizing issues of the depth aroused by this project drag out over many years, appointment to these boards may eventually hinge on support for, or opposition to, the project. In the company's view, over the nine years that the various proposals underwent review, state politics had led to a "balancing" of the local boards, with two members on one side, two members on the other, and a "swing" member whose vote had the effect of decision. Pressure on that individual could—and did—become considerable.

Polarization of membership did not occur so deeply at the county-review level. But there, too, the survival of the project ultimately turned on the approval of a single member of the board, and it was that member's attempts to avoid clear-cut decision by a "compromise" that scuttled the project in the face of extreme political heat.

The project failed ultimately in the company's view because it could not get local support for building new housing. Nor could it compensate for the lack of such support by gaining regional or state backing. Clearly there were people who would benefit—the construction trades people, who would get jobs out of the project, and the people around the metropolitan area who needed moderate- and low-cost housing. But the benefits could not be "localized"—they could not be attached to specific people. Construction trades people would build the houses, of course, but exactly which construction trades people would benefit, and for how long, was uncertain. It was even more difficult to identify specifically who would benefit from the newly built housing. So there was no active popular constituency speaking out in favor of the project, printing the leaflets, knocking on the doors, and waving the banners at demonstrations.

In contrast, the people who would be hurt by the project knew who they were: They were the people who lived in the area where the project would be built. They would lose their "playground." They would be politically submerged by the thousands of new settlers the project would bring in. They would have to pay the higher taxes to pay for the expanded local services that the "better-off" new settlers would probably demand. They might also have to cope with the effects of poorer

---

[1]Here, as in many other cases analyzed, company executives vociferously objected to "tax" money (i.e., government funds) being used to support legal services for their opponents. But this objection had no noticeable effect on either law enforcement officials or public opinion.

people attracted to the low-cost housing part of the project.[2]

There were no comparable values that the current inhabitants would gain from the project. Enlarging the regional housing supply was of no personal interest to them. Indeed, restricting the housing supply would serve to raise the resale values of the houses they already owned. In short, local people had no reasons to be agreeable or reasonable. And it became clear to all as the hearings proceeded that the company had no clout to encourage more "reasonableness" in the community. All it took was a little organizational talent and energy to tap this pool of interested people to do the work of organizing and demonstrating this opposition. The community organization repeatedly showed its capacity to get several hundred people out for important meetings.

The environmental issue emerges on analysis as something of a "red herring," a diversion that had tactical significance in affecting the arena of struggle. But environmentalism never had a strategic impact on the objectives or outcome. The rhetoric of environmentalism was used extensively to attract outside sympathy and contributions by all factions opposing the project. Much reference was made to "endangered species" of various kinds, often in statements that were proved to have little foundation in fact. But the rhetoric did have its usefulness for the community group. It absorbed the company's energies in countering the charges, and seemed to clothe the local residents' short-term and highly parochial interests in a broad metropolitan, statewide and, even, national interest in maintaining open lands—an interest in which local environmental organizations, notably the Sierra Club, joined. It is significant in this regard that the Legal Aid Counsel for the community organization, while carefully utilizing environmentalist support, was equally careful to dissociate himself and the position of his organization from environmental concerns.

The hearings procedures, which theoretically might have been used to insert the broader, long-range interest for house building to which the company was responding, was not successfully used for this purpose—and there is some doubt that it could have been. Environmentalists who examined the plan and found it acceptable, and even responsible, were successfully shouted down by the community people and their "no-growth" environmentalist allies.

The professional planners on the staffs of the various boards made no case for large-scale planning. Actually they took the reverse position, doubting the ability of county government to make such choices both because of its limited powers and because it lacked an overall plan of county and metropolitan development. Having been through many similar earlier hearings, they evidently had little faith in the ability of large-scale project plans to survive in the face of local opposition working through the local hearings procedure. Growth in the region, in their view, would "inexorably" be in the form of small-scale, largely unplanned "suburbanization."

Developing a Companywide Strategy

In the foregoing cases, companies are shown dealing with specific incidents and decision situations. In the next two cases, companies are also shown dealing with incidents, but the focus of the analysis is on the evolution of a companywide approach to dealing with the challenges posed by a politicized business decision-making environment. What should be clear from the analysis is that in neither case did the managements set out to systematically develop such an approach. Nor was the need ultimately to integrate public affairs planning into the business-and strategic-planning processes ever fully articulated. The cases, in other words, outline an essentially pragmatic adaptive process.

The Consumer Insurance Company: A Collaborative Effort

The company organized a consumer affairs department early in the 1970's, essentially to handle the complaints of its policyholders. From the beginning, however, the head of consumer affairs did a lot of reading, analysis, listening and conference attending with a view to ferreting out the trends in consumer organization interest that would provide issues for the company to decide.

One of the major issues then getting attention from consumer activists was the so-called "red-lining" procedure, whereby banks supposedly drew a red line around poorer areas on the maps of U.S. cities and refused to give mortgages or home-improvement loans to people in those areas. The policy was regarded as unfair to the poor, to slum dwellers, and to racial minorities, and became a source of protest incidents against U.S. banks in the early 1970's.

While consumer groups were not then attacking insurance companies on this issue, the company's consumer affairs department felt that "red-lining" was a potential issue for them as well, since the urban poor were also experiencing difficulty in getting insurance protection. Discreet probing by representatives of the company determined that insurance company "red-lining" was indeed on the consumer-activist agenda, and that the company had already been selected as a prime target once the activists had finished with the banks.

Seeking to head off the expected assault, the com-

[2]No overt mention of race or ethnic considerations appear in any of the reports of the case. However, there was community opposition to the government-sponsored low-cost housing requirements that the company incorporated in the plan.

pany's corporate consumer affairs department encouraged public affairs staff within the company's regional divisions to establish contacts with "responsible" local consumer groups. The move was only partially successful. The company's local public affairs staff were practiced in lobbying or in press relations. But they were not comfortable with people from the inner city, and not adept at dealing with them or with confrontation tactics. They saw their role initially as one of educating "these people, and telling them the facts of life." Additionally they felt: "This is a regional problem, so let's keep it in the territory."

But the local people were not interested in being educated. Local activists responded to the regional staffs by saying: "We know the facts of life; we get screwed by them all the time. You change your policy." The regional staffs found out that local groups were talking about issues over which regional division management had no control and which they could not change. As a corporate executive later described the situation: "They kept talking with the local activists and that was good. But they were reluctant to let their problems out of their territory for fear of being punished by corporate management for not putting their messages across. And that was bad. There are only so many times you can meet with a neighborhood coalition and tell them you can't do anything for them. Then things start to escalate."

Telegrams started arriving at the president's office. Tough letters arrived from a group of nuns who had formed a coalition, demanding the presence of senior officials at a meeting they were holding. A group appeared at the annual stockholders meeting, and demonstrated in front of the chairman of the board. "They red-lined the whole darned board meeting with red crepe paper," an executive recalled. "You can bet that got media attention."

Top management reacted to the demonstrations by rejecting the demonstrators as "the poor, the degenerate, and the real scum of society—people whom nobody would want for their business anyway." But the regional people, who had carried on local dialogues with neighborhood people, had come away with a different view. And, as the confrontation developed, these people pressed their view on corporate headquarters.

"You'd be surprised at these people," one report observed. "We came to these meetings expecting derelicts and instead met the Archie Bunkers of this world: People who have worked hard all their lives and are now caught on the fringe of something they don't want any part of. At the backbone of these meetings were angry white people, blue-collar workers who were furious at our inability to respond to their problems."

The company's regional division people were beginning to feel the spreading effects of U.S. economic decline and urban deterioration on their traditional insurance markets. There were more and more people the

company had once sought out eagerly for whom it could no longer supply insurance protection at a profit. Ultimately this had to affect the ability of the company to do business and grow.

At first the corporate reaction to the regional division people's reports was exactly what the division executives had expected. As one of them put it: "We didn't like the message, so we wanted to kill the messenger." But eventually, with the corporate public affairs department acting as a corroborating and validating agent, the message began to get through.

How was the problem addressed once it got corporate attention? As a first step, staff was deployed to take the following measures:

(1) The corporate consumer affairs staff worked through a coalition of counterpart staff departments in other insurance companies, attempting to persuade insurance industry leaders to sit down at the table and begin a dialogue with some of the national consumer leaders.

(2) Operations-oriented staff departments were alerted to the existence of the problem and asked for solutions. A major participant in this effort was the company's marketing department, whose underwriting practices were the source of much of the conflict. Their cooperation was essential in initiating any changes that might be made later.

(3) Eventually the product development department in marketing came up with a new basic homeowners' policy that would insure residences and household effects for market value rather than replacement cost. Introducing this new product eliminated a major problem of insuring in depressed areas. For, if a large apartment building is insured for replacement cost in a depressed area, it may well be worth more burned to the ground than if put up for sale.

"With the staff work out of the way, we were now ready for heavy negotiations," explained a corporate executive. The company's president joined with regional managers and other key local executives in meetings with local leaders. The president really only made an appearance at these meetings, taking note of the corporate desire to be responsive, "blessing the proceedings," and then often letting the regional people take over the meeting without him.

In these negotiations the company worked to develop an atmosphere for negotiation, in which information could be usefully exchanged. It was in this setting that community leaders finally recognized that business losses in depressed areas far outweighed premium intake, and conceded that there was a limit to what the company could do on its own. "We were already writing so much of the inner-city business," recalled an executive, "that forcing us to write more wasn't going to help anyone over the long run. Not when there were other liability companies who were not in the business at all.''

In an effort to get more insurance companies involved, the consumer groups now turned their attention to the state insurance departments, asking them to send representatives to the sessions. The state insurance representatives, in turn, brought in the other liability insurance companies. "A very good joint committee effort developed," remembers the consumer affairs executive, "which included executives from several companies, staff from the state insurance department, and local neighborhood leaders.''

The state insurance department examined each company's "book of business" to determine whether the companies were practicing unfair discrimination under state laws: (1) Was a company assigning people to the state-assigned risk plan who really did not belong there? (2) Did the company's marketing system give equal access to residents of inner-city and suburban areas? (3) Did company underwriters and underwriting practices apply the same criteria in inner-city and suburban areas? No "quotas" were involved, but eventually all insurers began to receive and accept more inner-city business. The state insurance department redesigned the state's assigned-risk plan so that it met many of the objections made by the companies and neighborhood groups.

The result has been a continuing system for handling inner-city insurance problems that links regional, corporate, intercompany and company-state government elements. "The thing to remember about the system," a company executive stresses, "is that it is problem solving—mutual problem solving—the identification and exploration of alternative solutions when one approach won't work. It's not an adversary approach.''

In some localities, where state or local governments lack adequate expertise and resources, the insurance companies have helped organize and support neighborhood service organizations. Executive directors of community organizations have been put through courses to give them a lay person's understanding of underwriting, so they in turn can give good advice to local people needing insurance. It is a system to help individuals through community cooperation with business and government.

In developing the system, the company found itself making a calculated attempt to get around the conventional adversarial approach with its open confrontations and legal maneuverings. "Being hard-nosed in public just has to affect your image," one executive commented. "Over a long period you develop real credibility problems with your own employees. They are disturbed to see people constantly marching around the building and having the company beaten up in the press. It's not good marketing. If you look down the road,

would our policyholders remain with a company that apparently isn't able to defend itself against all those charges?''

The strategy was to attempt to develop as an effective alternative a collaborative problem-solving approach. This involved the consumer affairs department early on in the development of contacts with community leaders and groups and with national consumer groups that were amenable to and capable of such an approach. The company would not deal with those who were seen as unable or unwilling to play in the collaborative effort.

Company people were trained and given practice in confrontation situations and negotiating techniques. Only people who received such training and who did reasonably well at it were allowed to participate in the collaborative effort. A company executive pointed out that: "There are terrific executives or technicians who just can't stand the fact that someone is actually verbally beating up on them. They just fold right in front of you. Others, who might not be such great executives, are absolutely beautiful in front of the camera or on their feet.''

Committees are organized in the company at regional levels, cross-functionally at corporate level, and interlevel (corporate and division) to coordinate the activities of company units and to facilitate planning and communication among them. These committees are designed to get individual problems quickly up to the company level where they can be solved. They are designed to focus attention on issues on a timely basis and give the problem all the expertise it needs. "The system allows us to assemble the right people with the skills to get a problem handled, and overall it gives us an early opportunity to see trends building.''

"Our objective was to build up greater sensitivity to the issue and its resolution," the consumer affairs executive explained of the reorganization "—and to reduce feelings of territorial protectionism about problems. We don't try to 'control' the environment anymore. That's the old thinking. Now we try to participate in it effectively.''

Responding to the Issues: The Case of A Bank

The successes and frustrations of one of the country's largest banks in dealing with external forces shows an evolving management attitude as to where and how these problems can be resolved. It also casts considerable light on what kinds of disputes the companies regard as intractable, and why this is the case.

Specific objectives—Many incidents aroused protests because the way the bank carried on its business injured a group or class. In this area the bank's executives' comments reflect a fair degree of satisfaction with what has been accomplished. As they see it, a major reason for this success is that the groups were able to identify definable objectives that the bank's executives could understand and do something about.

There may be disagreement as to the desirability of the protestor's objective, or of the means to achieve it, but the bank has no difficulty in understanding what the opposing organization wants, what its motives are for wanting it, and no real difficulty in giving the protestors what they want.

Organizational issues—A second type of issue that is more difficult to resolve because, in the company's view, the pressure group is not really interested in a specific objective. Its leaders have focused on the bank as a means of enlisting broad support for an entire program. "They merely used us as a punching bag," a bank executive complained of one protest. "There is no specific task to be accomplished or problem to be solved so the question arises: 'How can we deal with these people?'"

The answer is probably that negotiation and compromise are impossible. The company can only fight the new organization, accommodate to its wishes, or wait out the passage of its growing pains. In this situation where an organized entity is confronting an unorganized entity, where the protesting organization is still defining its objectives and trying to attract supporters, confrontations with companies are used not to solve problems but to build the organization.

Global moral issues—Some issues are pursued on a primarily moral ground. The protestors claim no personal injury to themselves or to any of the groups to which they belong. Rather they claim that some aspect of bank operation transgresses their (and presumably the bank's) moral principles. This kind of protest is felt by executives to be the most difficult of all to deal with. Often it is difficult to translate moral protests into achievable, concrete actions that a management can take. It is also virtually impossible to negotiate moral demands.

As the 1970's progressed, the bank found itself increasingly doing business in situations in which outsiders raised all of these issues. Two decision-making areas—doing business in depressed communities and doing business in South Africa—were mentioned by bank executives as being especially instrumental in framing this bank's thinking about how it could deal with outsiders generally. It is perhaps significant in this regard that each of these situations initially contained all three types of issues—"specific objective," "organizational" and "moral" issues and that the bank's ultimate sense of its success depended on the degree to which it was able to move the grounds of discussion away from moral and organizational issues to focus on specific issues that could be negotiated and resolved.

Community Issues: The Community Reinvestment Act

The bank's initial efforts to contain community issues were not successful and the repercussions were severe. One executive recalled: "Some years ago an order of nuns wanted management to put a proposal on the proxy solicitation which would have required management to allocate a portion of the bank's efforts to developing the ghetto. The response of senior executives who were planning the stockholders' meeting was: "We can't let outside groups tell us what we should do. Were we to do so there would be no end to the groups that would come forward and ask for favored treatment and involvement in our decisions."

Management urged the stockholders to vote against the proxy resolution and it was defeated. The nuns then enlisted Representative Reuss and Senator Proxmire in their cause and the ultimate result was the Community Reinvestment Act.[3] Clearly, stonewalling the group merely forced the protest group into other channels. In the view of a bank executive who followed out this line of thought: "This could have been handled at the beginning. What we forgot, and, indeed, have forgotten in other instances, is that social lobbying begets social legislation, which begets regulation—which, in turn, deepens and perpetuates itself. Now we have to deal with legislation that is rigid, cumbersome in its procedures, and loathsome in its secondary effects. We don't seem to be able to learn. We must learn to separate out the kooky from the reasonable issues, and to select the people we must deal with."

The Community Reinvestment Act, as passed, was more comprehensive than the original proposals, and, worse still from the company's point of view, mandates extensive research on the part of the organization to determine what its community is. And that is only the beginning.

As one executive speculated: "Once we have determined what our 'community' is, and what its needs are—no mean feat—I see the implementation of affirmative-action principles to banking. Suppose we cannot find qualified borrowers in the community, the government will then ask: 'What will you do to qualify the borrowers?' This may involve restructuring lending policies, or training people, or changing the repayment schedule, so that the interest paid by the borrower at the front end is lower."

Although in retrospect some officials might have preferred to accede to the original demands, most expressed general satisfaction with the way compliance

---

[3]For a review of experience with this legislation, see N. Weber, *Banks, Neighborhoods and the Community Reinvestment Act: Report on a Forum.* The Conference Board, Information Bulletin 85, 1981.

efforts have gone thus far. As one executive noted, a good deal of the process involves identifying who the real community leaders are and educating them as to problems of mutual concern so that, when a deal is struck, the constituents within the community will accept it. "These people have a lot of misconceptions about the bank. They think that because we are a large financial institution millions of dollars are at our disposal. They also think that we can wave a magic wand over a problem and it will disappear. They should know how circumspect we have to be in our relationship with legislators."

Another executive noted: "Over the years, I think that some of the more responsible people have gotten more realistic in their expectations. One of them especially, I believe, has a constituency that is not as sophisticated as she is. Sometimes you would like to rebut some of the things that she says, but I just let it slide. We can make a deal with her that will stick. I have never known her to renege. She takes extreme positions once in a while, but if you get her in a quiet moment and sit down and talk with her, a deal is at least possible."

Developing leaders takes time and the company had to be understanding and even help the process along. Speaking of the community organization's earlier days, an executive pointed out: "These groups were organizing a community, not necessarily rehabilitating it. It is an important activity. It is something that maybe we on the staff valued appropriately, and the bank's line officers ignored. As these groups became more sophisticated, as their needs became more clearly articulated, that is when the line's interest was more appropriate. So if they are now rehabilitating a multifamily building in their community, they need a banker as well as a grant officer. And we have been able to make that connection now, because the organizations are ready for it, because the problems are clearly articulated, and the role of government is more correctly assessed—and the problems with that role, and the failures in that arena. And that's why we are moving forward now in concert, as opposed to singly."

Even the information requirements of the Community Reinvestment Act produced unforeseen and beneficial effects. One executive noted: "Now we have an ability to sort down our files by geography, by zip, or by census tract; by municipality or state. Before the CRA we had not really spent the money to do that, but all the disclosure requirements of the government forced us to develop this ability. In certain areas I can tell where my problems are coming from and where my revenues are coming from."

Moral Issues: The South African Dilemma

There is one stubborn and intractable issue that will not go away—South Africa. Opposition to investment in South Africa is primarily on moral grounds; unlike community reinvestment issues, which may also have a moral foundation, accommodation by committing resources to individual projects is not possible. A company has basically two choices—it can agree to get out of South Africa, or it can stay there in spite of the opposition. Although that premise would seem to be an obvious one, it is surprising that most executives attempt to function in their day-to-day handling of the problem as though this is a more conventional issue—one for which some form of resolution of conflicting positions is possible.

The consequences of this failed perception (at least thus far) have not been disastrous. The bank continues to do business in South Africa, and there is little evidence that the external pressure groups have succeeded in broadening their base of support among shareholders. Furthermore, the level of confrontation has fallen off somewhat in recent years: One executive said that he did not recall any picketing on the subject since 1978. In addition, the bank does not seem overly worried about what is often *the* major concern in dealing with outside pressure groups—the fear that their response will lead to government intervention. As one executive put it: "South Africa is a classic issue of people who want something done that they *can't* get through government, and they *can't* get from the appropriate processes in Washington. And so they look for places where they *can* create visibility, or try to get that effect through the private sector or through other people. What they want is a total, complete boycott of South Africa by this country. And most of them that we hear from also work on Capitol Hill and in the State Department and have been trying to get that for a long time without success. The people in Washington who have the political responsibility to make those judgments can't rationalize the effect of a boycott on South Africa and on our own country in the whole scheme of the world situation."

If the South African issue does not represent a real threat at the present time, why discuss it? The reason is that it shows the limitation of potential productive exchanges between external forces and business—and these limitations are due in large measure to radically different perceptions and ways of analyzing the problem. A look at the bank's views on the South African situation also illustrates that the bank does (in extraordinary instances) employ moral criteria in some of its investment decisions. Although this has not resulted in avoiding South African investment opportunities at the present time, it does mean that certain situations are not considered appropriate. It would appear that the bank does not feel entirely free to operate independently of these kinds of considerations.

First, the differing perspectives—the bank attaches great importance to the many visits its employees have made to South Africa, and on "doing one's homework." Of course, first-hand knowledge and careful preparation are essential for a decision to lend money. It is not essential to the head of a church group who is making a judgmental statement. South Africa's racial policies are a matter of record—a church leader does not need to go to South Africa to develop further understanding. In fact, such a trip would be viewed as an unnecessary expense and an undesirable contribution to the South African tourist industry by the organization that he or she serves. Thus, a trip to South Africa is not only unnecessary for such an individual, it contributes in some way, however small, to the perpetuation of the evil that is being attacked.

Finally, the executives have difficulty in understanding positions that all agree will have little practical effect. For example: "If we pulled out of South Africa, nothing will change." Yet such a consideration is almost irrelevant, for the religious groups which, in this instance, simply want to avoid a connection with South Africa. If the South African system continues, regardless of their efforts, they want someone else to have the moral responsibility.

An executive described his bank's position as gradualist: "We do the best we can in a problem like this. If we can get twelve more blacks employed, if we make some progress, that's a gain." He contrasted his position with that of a church leader who said: "Whatever bloodshed it takes, whatever upheaval, it's worth it to correct this terrible condition and abuse. We have to have a total solution. We have to stand in solidarity."

Despite these radically different perspectives, the bank makes an effort to keep lines of communication open. One executive described his activities in this regard: "I would say that probably twice a month I have a meeting with a church group, a university, a newspaper, or some outside interest group about our activities in South Africa. And joining me in those meetings, I have someone from corporate communications because that is the way we have it set up. They are responsible for communicating our corporate activities to the outside. They are the professionals dealing with those issues."

Furthermore, the issue of South African loans is discussed by the board of directors. Reflecting on this practice, the executive said: "We do report to the board on a monthly basis any new or different developments in our lending practices in South Africa. I believe that's the only country we do that with. The board has discussed this issue at length. We have several board members who are very active in this issue. We have had several board members who have gone to South Africa."

For the time being, the emphasis appears to be on clarification, open lines of communication, and careful monitoring of activities by the board of directors. It is important to note, however, that the bank does not take the position that moral considerations are irrelevant, and these considerations can be significant in loan decisions. In certain instances, loans to governments are not per-

mitted. This is true in the case of South Africa, and one executive said: "We have verbalized the policy which we had previously—of not doing business with the Government of South Africa—but continuing to do business with those banks with which we had been dealing."

Loans for arms purchases are also avoided, if only on the grounds "that on a pure lending basis your risk is high." Iran's current government, for example, is talking about not honoring debts incurred for military hardware that was used to kill people who were against the Shah's regime. The bank also avoids countries, such as Uganda, where the social ills are "beyond anything we can tolerate."

The bank has developed certain moral criteria to which it resorts from time to time. It will not contribute to a government's attempt to perpetuate itself by force. While a country's level of human rights is seldom if ever a test for extending credit to a private borrower, the regime's commitment to improving the general welfare and living conditions of its people is important.

The South African issue is significant because it shows the limitations that exist as to potential cooperation and collaboration between business and external pressure groups. To a significant extent the clash between opposing views can lead to a constructive and final reconciliation. In some cases that is not possible—the issue of loans to South African businesses may be one of them.

Business Decisions and Public Affairs

In the give and take on substantive issues between business and its antagonists, companies often see themselves (and the institution of business) as powerless, while their opponents see them as virtually omnipotent. How can this paradox exist, and how can it be explained?

A company that is all-powerful in the eyes of those who stand outside its ramparts can expect that it will become the focus of rising expectations, and the target of hostility when these expectations are frustrated. As one executive put it: "Nearly all these pressure groups and pressures that come down on business are either (1) from something that business has been doing that was less than part of the populace thought it should be; or (2) from something a part of the populace wants done and can't get done somewhere else."

Few activists would disagree. Further, they would argue that their goals are desirable, and that American business is the institution most able to help achieve these objectives, or most responsible for the failure to accomplish those ends thus far.

This perception rests on the image of a monolithic leviathan that most executives find ludicrous. Whatever the awesome potential of American business in general, or an individual company in particular, executives are most aware of the limits to what an individual company, or group of companies, can accomplish. Yet business executives understandably prefer to focus on the positive side in dealing with their own employees and with the public, and emphasis on limitations is not common at sales or shareholder meetings. When a business organization then turns around and begins to focus on its own limitations such utterances are bound to be suspect.

What Business Can Do: The Limits

Business certainly is limited in what it can accomplish in bringing about change. As one bank officer commented: "The perception by people of how much business can do far exceeds *what* business can do. Business is just not smart enough to sort out a lot of these issues. Business, a corporation, is a dumb animal by definition. It has a lot of people, but it has a diversity about it that does not bring it to a single focus. It has a great deal of difficulty making up its mind about any particular issue, particularly if that issue has many facets to it. So the process is slow and costly. It has a determination to be absolutely right about what it does, which is a terrible handicap for someone who wants to deal with the political process in the public arena. So an advocate, or an activist, or a politician can run around the corporation sixteen times before the corporation can get its act together. Business has a terrible handicap in that respect.

"The company, by definition, is a political eunuch. It cannot vote, and cannot do any of the things that individual people may. But, at the same time, it has a concern and an interest as an entity."

While this individual did feel that pressure groups could be helpful as an "alert system" for the company on important issues, he also thinks that it is important for business to be aware both of its own objectives and of its limitations. Unfortunately, as he pointed out, this is not always the case:

"Business has been somewhat gullible in its response to these new pressures. Some businessmen have embraced these problems and almost made a career out of them, to the detriment of their corporation's business affairs. They have become so public-spirited and concerned that they have fallen prey to the things that labor union members used to complain about when their members would say: 'So-and-so has become a labor statesman, and is no good to us any more.' Some businessmen, I think, have also fallen into that trap."

Indeed, this individual felt that the need to reconcile so many conflicting interests before taking a stand on an issue is the fact that contributes most to the positive nature of a company's ultimate contribution to the resolution of an issue:

"The best thing a corporation has going for it is the judgment of a large group of decent people who have

diverse views, interests, connections and backgrounds. We should be working on developing mechanisms that integrate the corporate judgment into a good, more broadly based judgment. Better decisions result from all the adjustments and compensations that are necessary in the process of bringing together views from management, stockholders, employees, and so forth; they represent different interests.

"When you pull a judgment from that group—that each interest believes will succeed—there is a high probability that you really have a pretty sound judgment. That whole process is probably the greatest thing that corporations have to offer."

The question, then, becomes one of how a company institutionalizes and formalizes its procedures for responding to external groups. An individual with this responsibility described his own method of analysis: "There are three steps. First you identify the groups and the issues you can respond to. You have to think about the character of the issues and of the people involved. You have to differentiate between the issues that are reasonable and those that are not. It is also important to determine whether these conflicts are over facts or values. Where the issue is one of fact, and there is agreement on values, an accommodation can often be reached through a clarification of the facts.

"It is, of course, much harder to work out a resolution to a problem where the disagreement is over values. In these cases you have to assess the long-term as against the short-term costs to the company of some sort of settlement. When it comes to social issues, I think business people have difficulty in making a business decision. Pride gets in the way of a pragmatic assessment that would determine the true costs and benefits to the organization of a settlement. You only want to fight on those issues that will affect the basic character of your business, or where the costs of the battle are less than the long-term costs of accommodation."

To achieve the objective of evaluating the issues, along with the groups that raise them and the potential effect of accommodation on the company, the bank has established a public policy committee, of which this individual is chairman. The committee includes members of all the major operating and staff segments of the bank. This committee has a charter to identify issues which affect normal business activities in the United States and in foreign countries.

In line with this more positive and anticipatory approach, the committee chairman thinks that the bank should get involved in "advocacy advertising" along the lines pioneered by Mobil. In addition, the company's financial contributions should be used to support those causes that further its social objectives.

These approaches do not markedly distinguish the bank's methods from those of other organizations. This executive, however, is prepared to go further. He says, "I think that we ought to develop positions on social issues which are quite distant from the immediate operation of our business. Take the Equal Rights Amendment. You have to look at the alternatives to an amendment: Is a generation of court battles to establish the rights that the courts will quite likely grant to women anyway worth it in costs or benefits to society?

"I think that there is another way in which this formulation of our position in advance of any immediate impact can help us. We can build bridges to other groups by supporting their position when it is possible to do so. Not long ago the League of Women voters asked me for help in contacting cabinet members in connection with the Equal Rights campaign in this state. I felt the obligation to be helpful because we had taken a position on this. Since I was cooperative I would have no compunction about going to them at some time in the future for help on issues that concern us—like reform of the state banking laws."

Business as a Pressure Group

Where U.S. companies have differed most from firms in the rest of the world—and have been most innovative—has been where they have taken up the challenge thrown down by well-organized outside protestors to participate fully as a protest group in this more "democratic" political arena. An example of such "innovativeness" exists in the roles U.S. companies have taken in the "debate" over energy policy, and especially over what role, if any, is to be played by nuclear power in solving the U.S.'s energy problems.

Of course, energy policy has always been an area in which the U.S. government has played a hand. The power utilities are regulated. Many are state-owned. Gas and petroleum prices have been regulated by federal and state governments. Nuclear technology has always been regulated by the U.S. government, was developed largely under governmental sponsorship, and remains an area of intense governmental interest. But until relatively recently matters of energy policy and their regulation were matters resolved largely out of the public gaze among members of the administrative agencies, regulatory bodies, key members of Congress, and business lobbyists.

Nor were these political relationships all that overwhelming or important. Apart from the power utilities, which have been traditionally headed by lawyers, the heads of other energy-related companies—the oil companies and power construction firms, for example—have been headed by engineers, a reflection of the fact that energy policy stayed fairly stable for a long period of time, and embodied a stable division of labor between government and business in fulfillment of energy policy.

Whatever else OPEC has done, it has brought the old government-business relationship into question and made energy policy a matter of furious public debate. In the new environment the old approach has been derided as being "back door," and "under the table." Whether it is true, as its enemies charge, that the old way was "inherently corrupt"—or whether it was more efficient and logical, as its defenders assert—is really beside the point. For whatever its legitimacy, the old approach no longer works. Energy companies have felt they had "to go public" with their concerns, to cultivate the image and behavior of a "pressure group" among other pressure groups to get a hearing in the "pluralistic" and "fragmented" U.S. political scene.

There is no single business position, of course. In general, business executives have given a relatively high priority to gaining greater energy independence from foreign sources, with special reference to OPEC governments. They usually give special emphasis to stabilizing rising energy costs and uncertain availability. They generally see no single source of energy as being "risk-free," and no solution to the energy problem as all-encompassing or final. Hence, business executives' "solutions" to the energy problem tend to be multifaceted (involving development of many different sources of energy, relating to availability, cost and hazard in each application) and strategic (the energy sources changing as developing technology changes the cost, availability and risk equation). U.S. business thinking usually accords nuclear power a role in providing U.S. energy needs to the year 2000.

The energy-related companies have taken the lead in the public energy debates, with each industry and company adding its own particular wrinkle to energy policy, and having its own point of view. Power utilities have been extremely vocal in favoring the "nuclear option," or at least were so until the Three Mile Island reactor accident. Oil companies have been most vocal in defending the role of rising oil prices as an incentive to the development of energy supplies.

Arrayed against the companies has been a well-organized international (but largely U.S.) network of activist organizations. These organizations are generally regional or local in character, tied together by various national coordinating and information organizations of varying posture and effectiveness. Funding of the organizations comes from a variety of sources including the groups' membership, fund-raising activities of various kinds, private and family foundations, and government research and education grants.

The position that unifies the anti-company energy groups is a common antipathy to the use of nuclear power. Nuclear power plants are opposed on a variety of grounds including the charges that:

(1) Nuclear power plants present an inherently unacceptable hazard to the communities in which they are located;

(2) Radioactive waste from nuclear plants cannot be safely transported and stored over the long period needed for its decay into harmless substances; and

(3) The need to make nuclear facilities secure from terrorism and vandalism will lead to repressive governments that reduce civil liberties.

The anti-nuclear power groups favor a variety of alternatives. Some favor governmentally organized public-energy development companies. Others favor specific solar and wind technologies. Through all of these group proposals and actions runs an anti-business bias. The groups as a whole have reinterpreted the slogan of "energy independence" coined by President Nixon to mean individual independence from corporate power.

The tactics used by these groups are primarily informational and educational, with heavy emphasis being directed toward the media. Large public demonstrations have been held wherever nuclear plant construction has gone forward. The groups have been largely successful in utilizing such power plant accidents as have occurred to bring about a moratorium on nuclear plant construction in the United States. The energy companies, in becoming pressure groups in their own right, have developed their own set of tactical tools to counter these groups.

Issue programs: On certain selected issues, a number of energy companies have not only developed strong positions but have followed them up with "issue books" distributed to managers throughout the company outlining (in some detail) the company's position and the documentation for it. The books are designed to help the local manager deal with outside questions on the issue and to prepare speeches and press releases on the subject if the occasion arises. Often the company will have a speakers' program that encourages managers to accept speaking dates outside the company, and may coordinate speaking invitations.

Advertorials: The company buys advertising space in the local newspapers and time on television and radio stations to disseminate its political messages. Probably the best known of these programs is that run by Mobil Oil Corporation, which has placed advertisements about energy policy on the "Op-Ed" page (for "opposite-editorial," the page opposite the page on which editorials and letters to the editor appear) of the *New York Times.*

Opinion leader programs: The companies have designed and disseminated magazines, special periodicals, and personal letters to people regarded as influential in their communities at the city, state or federal levels, in the media, and the like.

Front groups: Energy companies have helped spawn and sponsor informational and educational groups favorable to their positions on energy policy. Such groups range over the spectrum of political activity, from research-types of organizations to those that sloganeer, march and counterdemonstrate, and even bring crude pressure to bear on individuals. During the period when the film "China Syndrome" was appearing in the movie houses and the Three Mile Island incident was prominent in the press, bumper stickers appeared on automobiles evidently financed as counter pressure by business-oriented groups. And when a large U.S. company decided to get out of the nuclear power business, its chief executive received a number of very critical letters from heads of power utilities.

As practiced by a number of the companies, the political struggle over energy policy is one in which a broad cross section of the companies' managers are expected to participate. The U.S. companies have been successful enough in pressing their views on energy and other issues for this pressure group-like activity to have become an issue in its own right.

In the Spring of 1980, for example, an array of outsider group interests—led by consumer and environmental activitists and their trade union and political allies—sponsored a "Big Business Day," the major theme of which was to focus public attention on the growth of company political activity and to protest the use of company economic power in this way. "Big Business Day" was regarded as a significant development by many of the U.S. public affairs executives interviewed, because they saw in it the first serious steps toward organizing the narrowly focused single-interest groups into a broad, anti-big business coalition.

But as a media event, "Big Business Day" got little news space and little editorial attention was accorded to its arguments. In the wake of the Republican victory in the 1980 federal elections, there is every indication that U.S. business intends to participate more fully in the public national decision-making process.

Chapter 3
Europe

TO THE BUSINESS VISITOR from abroad, Western Europe appears to be a collection of nation-states, each with its own distinctive legal and governmental institutions, its own language and culture, and its own historical memory. Of course not all of Western Europe's states are nationally homogeneous, or of long standing. Italy and Germany, for example, are relatively new states with significant regional-cultural and, in the case of Germany, deep religious divisions. Even so old a nation-state as the United Kingdom includes the culturally distinct Scots and Welsh as well as newer, racially distinct minorities from Africa and Asia.

Moreover, a variety of international and continental institutions bind the nations in various ways and somewhat dilute European nationalism. There are historic-cultural connections such as those that tie the Scandinavian countries together, that connect German-speaking European nations, and that tie Britain and France to former colonies on other continents. There are various economic communities, most significantly the European Economic Community headquartered in Brussels. There is a European Parliament, located in Strasbourg, whose members were popularly elected for the first time in 1978, and which represents a move in the direction of multinational political organization. There are the various Western European joint defense arrangements, such as NATO, that unite the western half of the continent.

The picture of Europe as a collection of culturally homogeneous states, however oversimplified, does provide contrasts with other regions analyzed in this study. The United States, although a single country, reflects the influence of many national cultures. Japan, on the other hand, although more culturally homogeneous than the countries of Western Europe, lacks their ties to a larger continental design.

The distinctive element about politics in these national states is that, culturally speaking, the people have "lived together" for a long time. Cultural, governmental and legal institutions have roots going back a thousand years or more. Social relations tend to cross institutional lines. European businessmen refer frequently to having known particular political figures since school or college days. In communities as homogeneous as those in Sweden, executives comment about having grown up with their union leaders in the community near the company and speak of socializing together.

The major divisions in European nation-states tend to be along social and economic class lines, divisions which can be exceedingly bitter but are usually national in scope and tend to cut across the major social institutions: the government, political parties, the military, corporate business, and the national church. Business people are less likely to be just business people. In France, especially, they may have once been government officials or university professors—and may be so again at some later period in their careers.

Legal and political institutions vary considerably from one country to another. Roman traditions of law exist in some countries. Anglo-Saxon common law in others. Local variations exist in all. But in nation-states, legal and political institutions tend to operate to some degree as the protector and promulgator of a majority culture.

The companies analyzed for this portion of the report tended to be smaller on the average than their counterparts in the United States. The median-sized U.S. company, for example, employed 40,000 people, while the median European firm employed under 10,000. Also, their business operations tended to be less far-flung than those of U.S. companies. More than half the European companies centered their business operations in one or a few countries, while 70 percent of the U.S. companies operated in "many" countries. Still, among the larger European companies analyzed are many—like Philips, Unilever, Shell, SKF, Ericson, Deutsche Bank, and Siemens—that rank among the world's largest and most internationally oriented firms and whose extensive multinational operations go back many years and exceed those of similar-sized U.S. companies. Thus reacting to outside pressures, they evidence a mix of narrow home-country concerns, accompanied by a sensitivity to the role of cultural differences in company operations and in the relations of companies to the outside world. There is, finally, an awareness and response to Europe's recent colonial past, in terms of the home country and company history, and also in terms of the wider European relationship to developing African and Asian countries.

The Character of Outsider Activity

Independent pressure group activities organized around special issues are relatively new to Europe. Historically, such interest-group activity has tended to exist as factions, or as "fellow travelers," of political parties—and this is still largely the case. In both France and Italy, for example, groups interested in social issues have tended to fall under the wing of large and well-organized Socialist or Communist parties and to be subordinated to party objectives. To this day, therefore, European executives point to unions and political parties as the primary sources of outside pressure on social matters.

However, increasingly, political pressure groups, whose interests focus on a single or a few social issues, have emerged in Europe as they have in the United States and Japan. Such groups have been especially active in Sweden, the Netherlands, the United Kingdom, and Germany. They tend to organize around a mix of community, environmental, energy and consumer concerns—as well as a number of more clearly religious and moral issues. Some of the major issues follow.

The close juxtaposition of plant facilities to residential centers was identified by a German executive as the source of three-quarters of his company's problems with outsiders over the past 10 years. The problem is a general one throughout the densely settled areas of Europe, but it is especially severe in Germany, where workers and citizens live close to major company facilities on a scale probably unmatched elsewhere.

The interspersion of industries in a landscape of greenbelts and residential areas was once regarded as a glorious achievement of German industrial planning. But, in recent years, the search for greater economies of scale has led to larger facilities in many industries. These facilities have become noisier and smellier, tending to overwhelm the communities in which they are located.

At the same time, local residents have ceased to look at the nearby plants as benign guarantors of jobs and prosperity; instead seeing the plant and its emissions as possible threats to their lives and health. To a younger generation which does not revere plant activity as a rescuer from the privations of depression and war, the noise and smells of plant processes are reasons enough to press for their removal to other areas. In the current environment, the expansion of existing facilities and the development of new facilities has proven to be a problem.

Opposition to nuclear power plants has its roots in the left-wing "Ban the Bomb" movements of the immediate postwar years. The movements have been strongest in Sweden, where a national referendum was held in 1980 on the issue, and in Germany, where massed protests and court actions have blocked power-plant construction. The impact of such groups has been considerable. Only in France, where the Communist Party has espoused the cause of nuclear power, has development of nuclear power plants gone rapidly forward.

Consumer issues have arisen on a wide variety of matters relating to product advertising, pricing and use. Indeed, lobbying on consumer issues has even arisen at the headquarters of the European Economic Community in Brussels, as well as within specific European countries. Consumer activism is of long standing in Europe. Consumer magazines are published in the United Kingdom, France, Germany, Norway and Iceland. Consumer information movements have been most active in Sweden, the United Kingdom, France and Germany.

Religious groups, especially national arms of the Protestant World Council of Churches, have pressed companies to stop their business dealings with South Africa. Such movements have been most active in Sweden and the Netherlands.

Anti-business groups tend to overarch all the above issues and groups. They tend to view environmental, consumer and other issues as additional evidences of the "bankruptcy" of business leadership, as further justification for radically reorganizing the economic system, and as a vehicle by which to gain more political power for themselves and their allies.

The Company Responses

European managements have traditionally declined to negotiate with groups challenging their behavior. Although sometimes sympathetic to the arguments of such groups, managements rarely acknowledge the right of outsiders to influence their decisions or concede to the principle of direct and formal discussions. At best, the views of outsiders might be heard informally, or would be received (and generally refuted) through an industry association or government department.

With few exceptions, managers seemed unwilling to accept external constraints on their activities other than those imposed by legislation or market forces. Corporate social responsibility took its guidelines from earlier concepts of aristocratic behavior. The paternalistic regard for employees and local communities did not require it to consult the objects of its charity, nor to consider the larger public in dispensing its largesse.

This traditional attitude has been much modified since World War II. Managers say they are generally far more open to argument and constructive criticism from outsiders than in the past. Managers themselves concede the existence of conflicts of interest that require them to be more responsive to the inquiries and demands of outsiders. Finally, business does not find government as sympathetic to business as in the past. On the contrary, government agencies and political parties frequently act as though they were the most powerful and aggressive of pressure groups, urging their own interests and views of the issues on corporate management.

A major change in the decision environment has been the result of attempts by national governments to bridge over social divisions in the name of greater national unity. These have attempted to draw employees into the decision-making process of the companies at various levels of organization. The major focuses of this effort have been the creation of works councils at the enterprise level, and the introduction of worker members on the supervisory boards of directors of companies. Depending on the home country and industry of the company, the experience of many managements with these devices goes back anywhere from ten to thirty years. In Germany, Sweden and the Netherlands, the inclusion of rank-and-file employees in the business decision-making process is not regarded as having been all bad. For, while most executives do not generally find the politicized decision process attractive, they do feel that it can be made to work and has, in fact, eased significantly the implementation of such perenially touchy business decisions as plant closings, permanent reductions in the work force, and changes in work processes.

The experiences have been favorable enough over an extended period of time for managements in these countries to attempt to develop closer ongoing relations with their unions on matters of broader social concern. This trend was observed most fully in Sweden, where surveyed executives went so far as to describe a national division of labor in which business takes the lead on economic matters and the trade unions lead on social matters. There are also efforts by a number of French managements to "learn from our German colleagues." They are attempting to establish ongoing communication and negotiation with non-Communist unions on both company and a union basis and through the national employer federation levels to resolve differences and to develop common ground on issues of mutual concern.

The attitudes that many European executives have developed as a result of these experiences, as well as the guidelines and techniques for dealing with them, have strongly affected the way these executives think about and deal with outsiders generally. Thus the thread of union-management relationship runs through many of the cases described later in this chapter, sometimes occupying the center of the stage of decision, always occupying a part of the background as each incident unfolds.

Fending Off Political Attacks

Europe's executives and firms take sharply different approaches to dealing with what they regard as politically motivated attacks on the corporation, and those "legitimate" grievances that seek to deal reasonably with a problem. An example of how a company handled such a politically motivated attack is supplied by the chief executive of a large German chemical manufacturer who, in this instance, handled the counterattack himself.

The attack followed several rail accidents in the United States during which tank cars containing dangerous gases were ruptured and inhabitants of towns in the vicinity had to be evacuated to escape chemical contamination. Alleging a similar risk from a local chemical plant, the environmental affairs official of a large German river city dramatized his case by issuing a booklet containing a map in which the chemical plant was made the center of a "circle of risk" that encompassed the entire city and its environs.

The mayor of the town, a personal friend of the chief executive of the company, raised the issue by telephone. The chief executive responded with an invitation to the mayor, to several of his deputies, and to the local chiefs of police and emergency services to visit the plant. Except for the mayor, the chief executive knew none of the invitees and carefully avoided any discussion with them before the meeting. Once on his own ground, however, the chief executive quickly got through the pleasantries and turned to the issues.

(1) *What is the history of accidents*? The chief executive asked the fire and emergency people: "During the more than 90 years we have produced on this site, have we had a plant accident in which any of the outside population had to leave their houses? Their answer: 'It never happened.' "

(2) *What is the comparative risk*? Still, both the plant and the town had grown over the 90 years, so a history lesson alone did not dispose of the visitors' concerns. Moreover, the chemical was produced and stored in large quantities at the site before being shipped, so the question of risk remained to be disposed of. Again the chief executive took the lead in the discussion, asking the fire and emergency people: "Suppose you are the pilot of a 747 jet airplane, fully loaded with fuel and passengers, but losing power and forced to crashland in one of three sites: (a) a football stadium; (b) the city square; (c) the chemical plant. Which would offer the least risk to the passengers and to the citizens of the city?" The fire and emergency people unanimously chose the chemical plant as the place to crash "if you had to crash." The public officials were amazed by an answer they had not expected, and now they took over the questioning. In defending their choice of a landing spot, the fire and emergency people cited the plant's lack of population concentration, the built-in safety features of the plant,

the safety procedures, the existence of security people and equipment at the plant, all of which would tend to minimize damage and loss of life and to limit the effect of the crash on surrounding areas. What had started as a confrontation between city government and company managers ended as a discussion among city officials.

The company's approach was fortuitous to some degree. It took advantage of the personal relationship between the chief executive of the company and the city's mayor. The choice of this approach was determined, however, by the decision not to deal directly with the maker of the charge but, rather, to use a political route in an attempt to neutralize him. It took advantage of the traditional cleavage between technical and political people in German society to assume that the public officials would not have spoken previously to the fire and emergency people in any purposeful way about the issues. Finally, it refocused the issue from one of "removal of risk" to an exploration of "comparative risk" in a way that made likely company allies out of the technically oriented fire- and emergency-services people.

"I repeat, I did not know these men personally," the chief executive emphasized. "I did not know what they would say. But I had strong feelings, based on experience, about how they would really feel about the irresponsible charges. I believed I only had to give them a chance to say what they believed."

A different kind of politically motivated challenge was posed by a series of free-swinging attacks on corporations appearing in books published all over Europe. Charges made against corporations in these books were often wildly inaccurate, even "libelous" in the strict legal sense of the term. One book, for example, accused a German chemical manufacturer of firing long-term workers after they suffered heart attacks; of paying new hires more than long-service employees; and of not following its own safety procedures. The truth was that the heart attack victim, whose story was chronicled, had not been terminated but moved to another job with fewer physical demands. The second charge was just wrong: Long-service employees were always paid more than new hires in the same job. While the third charge had some foundation in fact, the company's accident rate had fallen by almost 30 percent in the previous five years.

Faced with these kinds of charges, some European companies have brought legal cases for libel against the authors and publishers. Most have not, however. The chemical manufacturer, for example, decided against legal action, believing that even if the company won a judgment the trials would give greater publicity to the charges and would probably help sell the book. At the same time, charges could not be left unanswered. Where newspapers took up charges made in the book, the company asked for corrections by writing letters or by giving interviews. "We did not want it said that we had tried to suppress a book, no matter how false its charges."

The authors of the book then convened a kind of "tribunal" with the press in attendance to "hear" the charges made in the book. The company was invited but decided not to take part in the proceedings officially. Company management felt that to participate would be to "make this like an official tribunal, without affording the protections of law or knowing that we would get a chance to make an adequate statement. We told them, we make the rules or we set up the rules jointly." As if to give credence to the executives' fears, an observer sent to report on the meeting, was recognized by conveners of the "tribunal" and made a target.

The "tribunal" device was not regarded as particularly effective by the company. "In general," an executive explained, "people were sort of fed up with the tribunal device after that, and the issue petered out. I think one can draw some definite lessons from that. We might have gotten so involved wth the author of the book that we would still be a target every time something happened. That is what one of the book's targets did, and that is what happened to it."

The lesson these companies learned from handling challenges they regarded as "illegitimate" might be summed up as: "The less you have to do with these people, the better. Any information supplied, any discussion or compromise pursued will be used as a weapon against the company and its management."

Conciliation and Communication

However, according to most of the executives interviewed, "legitimate" challenges arising out of a desire to deal with valid, or at least reasonable, grievances against the company are best handled by early conciliation, communication, persuasion and compromise. Indeed, some European executives would describe a conciliatory approach as a "must."

A major German steelmaker said it learned this lesson when it decided to expand its facilities early in the 1970's in response to Japanese competition. The core of the problem was that the new technology had been developed in Japanese plants located far away from residential areas. It was too noisy to be borne by a residential population living only a few hundred yards away. A crisis was reached when lightning struck a transformer, cutting off electric power to the facility, and opening emergency safety valves. The sound of gases escaping through the valves compared to "50 jet planes roaring at 20 meters distance, for half an hour." Local residents brought action to have the facilities shut down.

When the plant had been built three years earlier, the company had gone through the existing procedure of reviews before various local inspection boards. In a process that took about a year, the local population was informed of the new technology. Information was given to the local press and other media. During construction, more information was handed out to the local press. So the company management was surprised when a local pressure group, formed after the plant went into operation, asked that the facility be shut down.

The group also extended its campaign into the newspapers, television and other media so that, after the episode of the lightning, they succeeded in pressing the local inspection board to issue an order requiring the company to reduce noise levels drastically by a specific early date or shut down.

Since the plant represented an investment of several hundred millions of dollars, and was a major source of product, a shutdown was deemed to be out of the question. However, achieving the required noise suppression would have cost the company several millions of dollars and affected its price competitiveness. So the company's response was to go to the courts for relief. However, the courts merely gave the company a little more time to soundproof its premises and, after going to courts, the company was pictured in the press as being uncooperative and unreasonable. Moreover, the court action provided a pretext for representatives of a local political party to come forward with a "compromise" that would have had the company relocating 1,000 families from the affected area. In the end, the company soundproofed the facility. The episode also led to stricter and more onerous review procedures being adopted by local government.

What lessons has the company learned? Under the company's new approach: "We would invite the neighbors to come into our works for an explanation of the situation; show them what we planned to do on the site in some detail; and give them figures to explain why we are doing these things." In these presentations the company would demonstrate an awareness of, and sensitivity to, the environmental issues presented by the new technology and would show substantively how the company planned to deal with them.

The new approach involves identifying the local "personages" and "power people" and assuring that they know the company's plans in advance and participate to some degree in the decision. Local political groups are brought in separately and asked for their suggestions and support. "The old way was easier," an executive observed. "The new way adds to your work and consumes your nerves. Because you have people on the other side of the table whom you don't like and who don't like you. Very often they have communist or socialist ideas. They talk in a way that is not very polite, and that displays their emotions. Often they are not open to argument and speak only in political slogans. Extremists are relatively few in number, but they have to be very carefully dealt with because they are always trying to sneak in and take over the group. When we are careful, however, they eventually show their real intentions to their own people and they are kicked out."

How far does a German company go in giving out technical information and negotiating with local community groups? As elsewhere, the choice is not entirely up to the company; the demands and interests of the local community leadership can be decisive. Industrial history plays an important role; the major industrial sources of pollution find themselves necessarily sharing more information and more technical information with outsiders, and generally having to be more responsive and accommodating to outsider questions and demands.

The steelmaker, for example, now emphasizes early on the technical details that demonstrate how clean and safe the new facility is, especially how much it exceeds local governmental requirements. But the company, in common with most of the European companies analyzed for this report, generally tries to avoid discussions of alternative technical solutions to environmental problems. Such discussions are believed to bring up issues of feasibility and cost that are regarded as proprietary.

Adversary Relations British-style: An Oil Company Sites a Plant

The European companies' view of tactics is strongly conditioned by the often-stated view that: "Companies are only a part of society. And we must not appear to dominate in deciding the larger questions of life and culture."

How this view translates into tactics is elaborated by a British oil executive in discussing how his company planned and implemented the development for a refinery plant and marine port that would handle North Sea crude oil output. "Our experience has taught us to worry about what I call the *juggernaut idea,* where you steamroll your way through. In that kind of situation you can win a battle and lose a war. The challenge is to get things done without making it look that way." The company must be seen to be responsive, willing to answer questions, and prepared to explain its views. But it must not appear too forward or too aggressive. Above all, it may not appear secretive."

In planning the refinery and port, the company attempted to learn from recent earlier and not totally successful experiences. Earlier plans had attempted to locate refineries close to markets for petroleum products in populated areas. In contrast, the new site was relatively isolated. "The nearest town was over three miles away. The two settlements in the area were a small village of two to three thousand people, and a New Town or dormitory town. Unemployment was running aground 23 percent. It was an area of land which had been earmarked by the local government for development.

"In the previous case we had tried to gain permission by slipping a bill quietly through the House of Lords. This sort of thing can (and in this earlier case did) react on you unfavorably. This time we were accessible to the public except, of course, once the public enquiry process had begun.

"What impresses me is that this thing, which was a major part of our strategic plan, could have gone either way. The lesson to be drawn from this fact relates to the planning process. You must remember that politics is for real, there is a considerable time lag on this long, drawn-out process, and you should not tie up too much capital too quickly."

In order to hear outside views, the onsite representative met regularly with individuals to discuss issues of mutual concern. The company was willing to talk to any number of people from one to one hundred persons.

Little or no opposition was raised to the refinery, due in large measure to the need for employment, but the marine facility proved to be a different story. The villagers raised environmental objections. It would interfere with recreation—sailing and walking—and the location was too near a 13th century abbey. The opposition demanded that the Secretary of State convene a public enquiry. "This was not our choice because it limits dialogue," one executive recalled, "but the groups wanted the enquiry and they got it."

In January of 1977, the public enquiry began. The procedure for an enquiry is similar to that in a court-room, with the major difference being that witnesses are not under oath. The core of the organized opposition, or so-called "action group," included approximately 25 individuals—and the company was impressed with the cool professionalism of its opponents—describing them as "credible businessmen." The "action group" focused on the marine facility because the communities wanted the work that the refinery could provide. As one executive put it: "Everyone wanted the bus, but no one wanted the bus stop."

At that point it became clear that the outsider group's resources extended beyond the boundaries of the community. A professor from the Massachusetts Institute of Technology testified in its behalf. "The amount of money being spent," as one executive said, "indicated to me that money—and more than a little money—was coming in from outside."

The company's major difficulty with a public enquiry was that, once the process was under way, it could not respond to allegations. "They had an advantage," one spokesman noted, "they could say anything they wanted and we could not reply. We are a worldwide company; we could not do anything that would be construed as an attempt to pressure the Secretary of State."

The opposition was not lacking in creativity or imagination. One of the most effective attacks came in the form of a docudrama about a tanker filled with liquid natural gas capsizing near the coast. As one executive recalled, "It was a very effective broadcast—like Orson Welles's 'War of the Worlds.' It sounded as if an explosive force 400 times that of the Hiroshima bomb was

perched right near your house. Little old ladies would call us asking 'what can I do?' It was a frustrating time for us."

In August of 1979, the government released its decision and the company obtained permission to go ahead with its plans, but the government added 56 conditions or "reservations" to the original plan. The opposition waited the full six-week grace period before filing its appeal—which was eventually denied. Once the decision was released, however, the company lost no time in getting its story out, using a representative on the site to respond to questions, and to inform the company of local sentiment.

On balance, one executive feels that both sides gained: "I was surprised at the degree of opposition and its effectiveness. There are advantages, though, to this lengthy process. If you take short cuts you have to live with them for a long time. I think that the opposition also gained. Our plan was approved, but with 56 reservations, and we had to form a liaison committee to work with them. They continue to have a say: We have to discuss all sorts of procedures, for example, whether we can send a lorry down a particular road."

The English executives felt they had done well in achieving even so complicated a solution. As one noted: "In the States you can sometimes pick three sites, play them off against one another, and see how it goes. In England, there are not that many suitable locations. It would be like inviting three girls out for dinner. Once the other two found out, they would tell the third and you would spend the evening alone."

Consumer and Product Use

European companies have generally had fewer protest incidents over the past 10 years than have U.S. companies, fewer pressure groups to deal with. As has already been demonstrated, this does not mean that European companies have not had their struggles. Nor does it mean that European companies have discovered any secrets that have not also been discovered on the other side of the Atlantic.

Most European executives appear to agree with their U.S. counterparts that the best way to win confrontational struggles is by anticipating and avoiding them. In Europe this has been accomplished by some approaches and devices that are very similar to those already examined that are used by U.S. companies. Other approaches are, if not unique to European countries, then at least more typical—and possibly more effective—there.

A case in point, both in its differences and similarities, is in the ways in which European companies have responded to what one U.S. executive described as the "increased interest in, and demand for, a diverse variety of information concerning products, services, safety, manufacturing methods, and company operations'' with informational programs of many kinds.[1]

Consumer movements take many forms in Europe. Over the past 20 years publications reporting on independent consumer testing of goods and services have appeared in the United Kingdom and Germany. Consumer education programs are carried on additionally in France, Norway, Sweden and Iceland. Much of this activity relates specifically to the use by consumers of company products. But in recent years the older consumer groups—joined by newer socially oriented business critics, trade unions, and political parties—have involved a number of companies in confrontations that require them to engage in public campaigns, unprecedented in the past, to make a case for the social utility of their products.

In both Sweden and the United Kingdom, for example, companies preparing to introduce disposable bottles found it necessary to explain to the public, in articles prepared for the media, in press releases, in advertising, in public meetings, and in political forums, why these bottles were socially preferable to reusable bottles. In doing so, the companies drew attention to the existence of the whole chain of production and distribution operations that made the "one-way bottle" a socially responsible product and not just an economically attractive distribution medium for manufacturers. The programs aimed at the public emphasized energy savings rather than cost savings, focused on the entire production-distribution chain—not just the parts of it that would interest a food bottler—and focused especially on the parts of the chain that are invisible or inconspicuous to the consuming public.

The companies, while conceding that more energy would be consumed in producing the new plastic bottles in a "nonreturnable distribution environment," stressed that energy formerly used to gather and resterilize glass bottles would be saved. Also plastic bottles are lighter than glass, are cheaper to ship, and are less prone to damage. The objective of the companies' campaigns was, of course, not merely to persuade the public that buying items in disposable bottles was a responsible action, but to "fend off the efforts of politicians to put restrictions or taxes on the product," restrictions which might have eliminated the economic advantage of manufacturing plastic bottles.

Another device for anticipating and avoiding conflict—and again, one that is not unique to Europe, but has been especially effective in many countries there—is what might be called the "national task force" approach.

[1]Dorothy Holland, Vice President-Consumer Affairs, Kraft Incorporated in *Consumer Protection: Implications For International Trade,* edited by E. Patrick McGuire. The Conference Board, Report No. 789, 1980, p. 19.

Such national task forces go by such names as committees, Royal Commissions, Commissions of Enquiry, and the like. They may be formally established by governments after major problems have surfaced and been identified, or they may be highly informal and unofficial exchanges of views very early on in the development of an issue. A Swedish food company executive observed: "The typical, almost reflexive, approach to dealing with an outstanding social problem (in Sweden) is to take up the telephone and talk to all of the people involved."

The relative cultural homogeneity of many of the countries of Europe tends to encourage such collaborative, cooperative approaches on a nationwide basis. The process is described as one of "national" decision-making during which all the parties and interests are gradually identified, and the issues framed. Commented one asbestos company executive: "We would never think to take an agency of government to court. We would try to influence each other to do the right thing in direct negotiations and discussion. We would try to arrive at a consensus as to what was fair and reasonable."

How such collaboration works to ease and regularize relations between business firms and government over an extended period of time can be illustrated by the history of the development of British asbestos regulation. In this development outsiders have played an extensive role over the years, but open conflict and protest has been at a minimum. The first British asbestos regulation became law in 1933, the result of continuing close cooperation between asbestos manufacturers and users and government occupational medicine researchers. At the time there was a general agreement that the problem was a matter of a progressive decrease in lung function (called asbestosis) caused by prolonged exposure to asbestos dust. Accordingly, the 1933 legislation required that dust be eliminated from factories and working spaces.

By the end of the 1930's, there was a growing suspicion among medical people that asbestos was also connected to some forms of cancer, but methods for measuring exposure and assessing risk were lacking. It was not until the 1950's that the suspicions took a more concrete form as an expected drop in the incidence of asbestosis was not taking place despite the anti-dust regulations. "Government safety inspectors have easy access to company executives," a British executive explained. "If they are upset about something, we, of course, have to do something about it." This led to an agreement between companies and government to develop new methods of collecting, classifying and measuring various types of asbestos and fiber dust. The work was done largely by company people.

By the early 1960's, researchers arrived at the conclusion that the source of the problem was ultra-small mineral fiber, particles of which became lodged permanently in the lungs. Of these ultra-small fibers, one type of a particular ratio of length to width (the so-called "long thin" fiber) evidently further damages lung cells in ways leading to lung cancer. It was concluded that after forty years of work exposure to air which contained two of these long-thin fibers per cubic centimeter, one percent of the population would develop a particular type of lung cancer known as mesothelioma.

Outsider interest emerged at that time in the form of occupational environment activists who attempted to end the use of asbestos. Asbestos companies say it is impossible to keep people absolutely safe, that asbestos fiber is everywhere in the environment at concentrations equal to or above the regulatory standard. Moreover, they allege the danger is not from asbestos fiber alone but from any "long thin" mineral fiber. Other available mineral fibers that might be used to replace asbestos are at least equally dangerous, they say.

In 1976, the process had gone far enough for a committee of enquiry to be established by the British government and charged with proposing recommendations for dealing with the problem. The committee included three industry members, one of whom was a builder and one an asbestos company executive. Three members were from the unions, of whom one was from the construction workers union, and one from the textile and allied workers union (whose members work in asbestos factories). There were two industrial hygienists, one from the Royal Navy and the other an academic; three medical doctors; and the deputy chairman of the Consumer Council, a private group that deals with various consumer issues, particularly those of interest to the housewife and involving the management of the household.

The committee of enquiry had every expectation that most of its recommendations would ultimately either be enacted into law or would form the basis of company regulation. One member of the committee commented: "We carried a weight of public expectations that led us to act in a responsible, expeditious and cohesive manner." The final report of the committee was submitted without dissent in six months. Dissents occasionally occur in the reports of committees of enquiry, but the object is a consensus. Dissents are not to be used to express private points of view nor to develop negotiating positions, but to indicate where the work of consensus was not accomplished. "Frivolous" dissenters run a risk of losing credibility for their ideas and themselves with "people who count," an executive noted.

As a member of one such group explained it, industry members are supposed to function as though they are members of the public, considering and seeking the objectives that benefit and protect the general public. At the same time, they are supposed to represent the industries and companies from which they come.

Industry members usually assess at an early stage the issues to be explored and likely positions to be taken by the committee at the end of its deliberations. They inform their superiors and peers from other companies in the industry who are not on the commission. As such, the industry member becomes a representative, drawing on ideas for committee consideration from industry and company figures who are not actually on the committee. An intimate observer of the process notes: "The industry member generally finds himself ticking his industry to progress faster, while restraining government and public figures who see none of the difficulties and who want to move very quickly indeed."

The asbestos committee of enquiry made 41 recommendations, of which 36 were immediately accepted by industry; two were accepted with reservations related only to timing (the companies wanted two additional years for implementation); and three became the object of controversy. The recommendations found wide acceptance outside the United Kingdom, the one fiber per cubic centimeter standard being accepted by both the European Economic Community and the Occupational Safety and Health Administration in the United States.

The committee of enquiry approach is not without its problems. Participation on the committee was no absolute protection against the inclusion of utterly unacceptable recommendations. One such recommendation— the banning of Chrysolite asbestos (industry favored the regulation of the materials used rather than its outright ban)—was included in the final report.

A second problem arises out of the fact that, in the industry view, the committee of enquiry did not recognize its own limitations. The fact of widely inclusive membership—and the injunction of the government to the committee to take a broad public view—could have led a committee to bolder recommendations than a more modest charter and membership might have allowed them to do. By banning Chrysolite, for example, the committee of enquiry was felt to be placing British companies under a disadvantage when competing with French and Italian companies in the Common Market.

Putting together national task forces, moreover, can pose other problems for smaller countries. Swedish executives noted that the tendency to deal with every problem by such task forces and committees has the ultimate result of forcing a kind of convergence of thinking on social issues. Often people have served together on so many different groups that they come to understand the positions of the people with whom they will ultimately serve. This may narrow the range of choices on solutions to problems.

Dealing with the Unions

In Europe the most significant nongovernment "outsiders," as managements see it, are the trade unions.

The same estimate could be expected from U.S. executives, but where U.S. labor unions limit their role largely to employee pay, benefits and working conditions, European executives tend to see the labor unions as playing large roles in all social matters affecting the company's relation to society.

This social role has developed most markedly in countries like Sweden where unions may, by law, negotiate with employers about virtually any matter of social concern—including the company's policies in South Africa. It has not gone nearly so far in countries like France, where trade union representatives recently attempted unsuccessfully to negotiate with the "Patronat," the French employers' association, over such consumer matters as pricing, advertising and product quality. Somewhere between the two extremes are countries such as the Netherlands and Germany with "codetermination" laws of various kinds that actively bring workers' representatives into board-level decision making and introduce worker influence into middle level decision making through the operations of works councils. In the United Kingdom, unions wield power as the single most important element within one of the two major political powers.

It should be stressed, of course, that the primary concern of trade union members and employees is pay, jobs, pensions and working conditions, and this is no less true in Sweden, for example, than it is in the United States.[2] Yet the Swedish unions and their national leaders have played significant integrating roles in Swedish politics on social matters bearing only peripherally on traditional labor issues. When the issue of what roles, if any, Swedish companies were to play in South Africa first surfaced in the late 1960's, it was a religious and moral issue and had little to do with unions. Letters of inquiry were circulated by the Swedish Lutheran Church to companies with business operations in South Africa. These letters took a basically reformist approach, aiming at betterment of working conditions in Swedish-owned facilities as a means of leading to improved employment practices and working conditions throughout South African industry.

The unions only came into the issue strongly after the churches, feeling that it would have no effect merely to open job opportunities because blacks lacked skills, added a demand for training to their programs. This program became a major agenda item at an international meeting of Trades Unions in Brussels in 1973. The Swedish union movement, on returning from this meeting, came into the issue "very strongly," in the words of an active union participant.

A study commission of trade unionists was dispatched to South Africa the following year. It issued a "study report" on its return that formed the basis for company-trade union negotiations with Swedish multinationals operating in South Africa.

The union's most significant "demand," according to a number of Swedish executives, was a push for black unionization. But its role has not been clear or constant. For example, the original union study delegation had decided on its return to hold annual updating sessions to evaluate progress. But it actually met only once afterward. Some individual unions have made one or two follow-up visits to determine how solid the progress toward unionization has been, and to see to what degree job opportunities for blacks have increased in Swedish companies. Some companies also report that their local unions continue to monitor the progress of unionization in South Africa. But executives tended to feel that, in general, the Swedish labor union movement had lost much of its momentum, if not all of its interest, in the issue.

The reasons for this decline in momentum are seen variously by Swedish executives as lying in:

(1) The country's economic problems: "Recent years have not been good ones for the local company," an executive explained. "Local workers are dependent on the South African market for their jobs."

(2) The trades union movement has itself split between the reformers and a "radical wing" that wants companies to leave South Africa.

(3) Finally, and perhaps most significantly, the issue has become political—the subject of party programs and government legislation. Legislation passed by the Swedish government in the past several years lays out policies for Swedish firms operating in South Africa, and sets up reporting procedures to measure progress.

Nevertheless, the companies analyzed continue to regard the issue as an active one and the union role as a continuing factor in its evolution. One company, for example, which is following a policy of reforming working conditions in its South African subsidiary, feels that a close relationship with the Swedish union is significant to the policy's successful implementation. The union is seen as "a valuable source of intelligence and a useful corrective" to staff reports on the implementation of the policy. Some of the companies see the union role as buffering them against the demands of more extreme groups, and especially those of the churches. As one executive explained it: "We have found it appropriate to let the union tell the world what we are doing in South Africa. Of course, we also have our say. But we have learned that they are far more credible. When the world hears the facts from the union it believes them far more than if the same facts came from us."

This same "buffering effect" where unions and em-

---

[2] Recent economic reverses in Sweden have tended to reemphasize this truism, threatening the long peaceable working relationship between Swedish business and the unions. Sweden had its first significant strikes since the 1930's in 1980.

ployee associations have been brought into decision processes has been noted in other issues besides those of South Africa, and outside of Sweden in countries that practice some form of codetermination. A German executive noted that: "We have always wished that our employees would consider the economics of the business in making their demands. As members of the Oversight Board it becomes their duty to do so. They become very effective representatives for the company before groups of outsiders and members of the Social Democratic Party. They are very useful in helping us decide whom we must listen to and who are simply the crazy ones."

Acting as a Pressure Group

For all the emphasis that European managements place on taking the "low profile" there are clearly times and issues where managements have taken very active public relations stances. One such instance has already been explored in the reaction of the British oil company to public opposition to its Scottish coast facility. In that instance, however, the company deliberately chose to take a minimal stance, choosing to answer charges, being deliberately reactive rather than active and aggressive in dealing with outsiders.

In recent years, however, more European companies have chosen to take aggressive leadership positions in their countries. These more active positions, in which companies chose to become pressure groups that affect public opinion, have arisen in instances where managements felt their survival—as companies, as industries, and as part of a system of private enterprise—was at stake.

Such activity appeared all over Europe. Even German firms, in dealing with opposition to the construction of nuclear power plants, have found themselves engaged in active public debates and information campaigns. But it is in the Netherlands and Sweden that the research for this report found the most active questioning of traditional reactive approaches to outsider activity. After their success in the Swedish Referendum on Nuclear Power, a company leader wrote: "Experience from the campaign has led members of the business and industry organizations in Sweden to consider whether information programs can be conducted exclusively in accordance with the traditional pattern that has prevailed to date: by concentrating on decision makers and mass media. The question has been raised whether the general public does not also have to be informed and made aware of the conditions under which business and industry operate."

Becoming an effective player in the political campaigns of the European nation-states requires, of course, a sensitivity to local conditions and requirements. But companies from a number of countries found some common themes.

A number of companies, for example, have embarked on campaigns of "demystification." "In the past," a public affairs executive explains, "our company was secretive, explaining little to the public, giving out as few facts as possible." Another executive, from a country several borders away, amplifies: "We tried to project an aura of mysterious and unlimited power. Our owners felt that would make outsiders admire us, fear us, and want to deal with us. Potential enemies would be discouraged and would have no idea how or where to attack us."

"Our perceived omnipotence has become a problem for us," a British executive commented. He pointed to an item in a London newspaper in which a young woman had sued a local English utility for "almost magically" neutralizing her contraceptive during a power failure and causing her to become pregnant. In a more serious vein he pointed to the thrust of "Big Business Day" in the United States, and of moves to nationalize major Swedish banks as generated by perceptions of corporate secrecy, conspiracy and omnipotent power.

In anticipation of greater participation in the more democratic decision-making environment, these companies have mounted campaigns designed to reduce the company to more human dimensions, to clarify what the company does both in its economic and social roles, and to emphasize the limit of its roles and powers. Faced with the recommendation that his company pursue such a program, one aristocratic European executive objected, declaring it to be against his political principles. But he went ahead with the program.

Such programs of demystification have taken many forms familiar to public affairs departments the world over. In Sweden, the towering, fatherly figure (both literally and figuratively) of Marcus Wallenberg, chairman of Skandinaviska Enskilda Banken, went on Swedish television in a series of low-key interviews aimed at explaining and humanizing the Swedish banking industry. In The Netherlands, Philips opened its facilities to a well-known documentary film maker of Marxist orientation, hoping thereby to gain greater attention and credibility for the "facts" of company operation.

In acting as public pressure groups, however, companies in Europe are very concerned at the idea of appearing to use corporate power to overwhelm their opponents. A British executive observed: "If we allow our confrontations to turn into contests between corporate Goliaths and pressure group Davids, we will always lose. Even if we win in the short term, we will eventually lose in the larger scheme of things."

Viewed from this perspective, therefore, the Swedish Nuclear Power Referendum of March, 1980, though unsought by Swedish companies, turned into a distinct opportunity for public opinion formation. As in many of the countries of western Europe, the issue of the use of nuclear power arose in Sweden during the 1970's. The issue took on distinctly Swedish overtones, however, in that Sweden, always lacking in fossil fuel sources of her own, had early turned to hydroelectric power and, in the 1960's, to nuclear power. Nuclear power became a political issue in the early 1970's when an antinuclear stance was adopted by the parties outside the ruling Social Democratic-dominated coalition—the right-wing "Center" Party and the far-left "Communists." The 1976 defeat of the Socialists—the first in 40 years—was ascribed at least partially to the Center Party's antinuclear stance, and opened a period of continuing public debate and dispute over energy policy.

The Center Party early called for a referendum on nuclear power, a move opposed by the Social Democrats. For, while referenda only have a consultative function under the Swedish Constitution, the broad mandate they create can effectively bind the hands of government. In 1978, the Center-led government collapsed on other issues and the government that replaced it slowly reversed the antinuclear policy, developing a new policy that allowed "cautious" expansion of nuclear power. The referendum idea seemed dead.

Then, in March, 1979, the accident at the Three Mile Island nuclear power plant destroyed the Socialist-built consensus, and the Socialists were forced to abandon their opposition to the referendum. As described by a Swedish science reporter, Per Ragnarson:

> "The [March, 1980] referendum marked the culmination of a nearly 10-year-long public debate which had shifted from specifically scientific and technical problems concerning the environment and nuclear safety to more general ethical and moral issues concerning what kind of society Sweden wanted to create in order, hopefully, to guarantee itself a secure economic future."[3]

Three alternative approaches to nuclear power were listed on the referendum. All three viewed nuclear power as an interim source of power to be used until alternative power sources could be developed. The most "pro-nuclear" alternative—the so-called Alternative One—formulated by the Conservative Party read:

"Nuclear power is to be phased out at the rate that is possible with regard to the need for electricity for the maintenance of employment and our welfare. So as, among other things, to reduce our dependence on oil, and until renewable sources of energy become available, at most the 12 nuclear reactors which are now in operation, completed or under construction, are used. There must be no further expansion of nuclear power. Safety considerations are to determine the order in which the reactors are taken out of operation."

[3]From an article by Per Ragnarson "Before and After: The Swedish Referendum on Nuclear Power," reprinted in *Political Life in Sweden*, September, 1980, by The Swedish Information Service, 825 Third Avenue, New York, New York, 10022.

The second alternative—the one promulgated by the Social Democratic party and supported by its allies—was the same proposal with some additional conditions that encouraged government to:

- promote energy conservation;
- accelerate research and development of renewable energy sources;
- increase safety and oversight precautions for each nuclear power station;
- avoid oil and coal power stations as alternative energy sources (to reduce the danger of pollution);
- put production and distribution of electricity in public hands;
- prohibit the installation of electric heating in new permanent structures.

The third alternative—regarded as the anti-nuclear alternative—and supported by the Center and Communist parties would have:

- phased out the six reactors currently in operation over the next ten years;
- placed greater emphasis on each of the conditions of Alternative Two, including the proviso that reactors be shut down if "current or forthcoming safety analysis so require..."

Clearly, representatives of the Federation of Swedish Industries, led by the nuclear power machinery producers and power utilities, would have preferred no referendum at all. Like the Social Democrats, they were concerned at the prospect of being "locked in" to policies that events and technological change might render unfeasible. They were especially bothered at the prospect of being limited to 12 power plants. However, the referendum did offer a definite opportunity to end the public squabbling over energy policy and to get a national decision on the matter. Moreover it set up a situation in which business could make an active defense of its position.

Swedish industry and business interests did not pass up the opportunity. A "Business and Industry Energy Information Group" was set up by The Swedish Employers Confederation, the Swedish Association of Power Companies, and the Federation of Swedish Industries. To chair the working group, an executive of the ASEA Group was named and other executives, mainly from the most affected industries, were put on loan to staff the organization.

The high-profile campaign was organized into five working units:

(1) a unit dealing with opinon analysis and evaluation of policy issues;

(2) a "fact bank" devoted to production of fact sheets, small leaflets, and other specific projects of a mass information character;

(3) a mass media relations unit dealing specifically with national press;

(4) an editorial production and distribution unit;

(5) an "Energy Promotion" unit, which organized regional conferences, developed and trained regional groups of local company managers, and did local press relations work.

Overall, the scale of business effort was unprecedented. Over three million fact sheets alone were distributed in a country of only about eight million inhabitants. In addition, every form of informational activity was brought into play—including books, films, television shows, conferences, teaching cassettes, pamphlets, streamers, press releases, newspaper advertisements, and billboard advertisements.

Nearly 75 percent of the adult population eligible to vote actually took part in the referendum. Children took part through straw polls in the schools, bringing to perhaps 90 percent of the total population the percentage involved in the referendum. Opinion surveys showed a high level of popular interest, and one that shifted steadily during the campaign toward a more moderate stand on the nuclear issue. In the voting:

- Alternative No. 1 received 18 percent of the vote;
- Alternative No. 2 received 41 percent of the vote;
- Alternative No. 3 received 38 percent of the vote.

Business executives, while hardly overjoyed at the outcome, expressed some satisfaction with the fact that the first two alternatives taken together—which allow a "cautious" mandate for continued nuclear power development—garnered a sizable 59 percent of those voting.

Chapter 4
Latin America

ASK ANY LATIN AMERICAN business leader what is the most significant external force with which his or her company must deal, and the answer will most certainly be *government*. This is true regardless of whether the individual comes from a country governed by an authoritarian right-wing regime, a left-wing dictatorship, or a popularly elected parliamentary government. Indeed, with the exception of Mexico, business leaders in most other Latin American countries have had to deal with more than one of these different kinds of systems (or variants of them) over a period of years.

Argentina is a good example of a Latin American country that has had many different kinds of governments since World War II, and one executive summarized this view of government as the only persistently intrusive force through a long period:

"My business experience of 33 years is confined to Argentina, and while I can assure you I have seen a lot of *governmental* pressures on private corporations, there are not enough instances of 'nongovernmental outsider influences' to permit some generalizations about Argentina that could be meaningful to the international business community. I have the feeling that the main pressures on private business in Argentina have come from the government sector itself, and that most of the issues have come to the light of public debate through the interplay of government forces and private business organizations."

The Latin American experience is different from the others. With relatively few exceptions, it is concerned with efforts to accommodate government, all kinds of governments—democratic, authoritarian and socialist. The existence of government as an external force which is intrusive to a degree that is unknown in other regions transcends ideology and is rooted in history and social custom. Although government is the preeminent and, in some countries, the *only* external force with which

business must contend, there are many different kinds of governmental interference which should be distinguished at the outset.

In the first instance the government exerts pressure on a company to engage in, or to refrain from engaging in, a particular activity. In this case, the government is serving as a conduit for pressure which has been exerted on it to achieve some sort of objective. Most of these cases involve labor unions or rival business associations. The practice is for these groups to go directly to the government, and not to confront the company first.

The second example is where the government acts directly on its own motion and without any prompting from pressure groups. Businessmen attribute this "rogue elephant" behavior to the residual paternalism in all forms of Latin American government. Suffice it to say, a government that acts on its own and not in response to pressure (even though it may be a democratic government) is a novel one. Yet Latin American governments do this all the time for a variety of reasons. A far from exhaustive list of such motives includes: (1) a desire to achieve some sort of accommodation with a foreign government; (2) the government's perception of the country's economic necessities in a period of rampant inflation; (3) the belief that minimal standards of American food and drug safety should be implemented by decree in their own country; (4) economic nationalism; and (5) corruption.

The third example of government impact on decision making is where the government is a competitor in the particular industry in which the company is engaged, or where it chooses to enter that industry as a rival. Competing with the government is an unusual situation—in most other regions an industry is wholly public or wholly private, but Latin America has many examples of industries in which companies are in direct competition with the public sector.

Finally, there is the situation where government is the other party to a contract with a company. When this is the case, firms are confronted with a customer or supplier that has immense bargaining powers.

So when the Latin American business executive says that the dominant (and in some cases the only) external influence is government, it does not mean that Latin American business is free of the burdensome intrusions that exist in other countries. The issues which arouse passionate concern in other regions (e.g., environmentalism, feminism, etc.) may be of lesser, or even no, concern. But if the Latin American experience proves anything, it is that governments of all ideological stripes will find a reason (or, in some cases, need no reason) for active intervention in the business process, regardless of whether or not a constituency is actively urging it to take this course.

The primacy of government means, for the most part, that other pressure groups are significant to the extent that they can move the government to act. In this regard only two kinds of organizations are important: (1) labor unions, and (2) industry associations.

With the exception of a few recent occurrences in Brazil, labor unions rarely opt for direct confrontation with companies. Thus, in most instances, while a demand may originate with a union, it is only a concern to the extent that the union has enlisted the government's sympathy. This is equally true of industry associations, which generally attempt to persuade the government to move against a company—rather than confronting the company directly. Thus unions and industry associations need only to be taken into account by companies to the extent that they are able to get the government to adopt their position against a rival company or industry association. Table 4 shows which pressure groups are thought to be significant by Latin American respondents, and Table 5 illustrates the contrast between the Latin American view on the importance of government and that of the European and U.S. business person.

Government is certainly a factor to be reckoned with in all three regions—a majority of the American respondents, and an even larger proportion of Europeans, felt that "government was usually more important." The view with which nearly three out of four Latin American participants concurred—that government was *always* more important—was not the prevailing sentiment among Americans and Europeans.

The importance of government as an external force that must be taken into account when making business decisions in Latin America does not mean, for example, that environmentalism is not a force with which a Latin American company must contend. It means, rather, that there is little or no direct confrontation in Latin America of the kind with which Americans and, increasingly, Europeans have become so familiar. Of course, many Latin American business leaders felt that it was only a matter of time before many of the *issues* raised by these various pressure groups—environmentalism, feminism

Table 4: Pressure Groups Having Significant Impact on Latin American Respondents (26 companies responding)

Group	Number Noting Significant Impact [1]
Environment.	4
Unions.	16
Political parties	10
Women's or feminist groups	0
Minority, racial, nationalist, ethnic groups.	1
Handicapped groups.	0
Religious groups	2
Consumers groups	2
Ad hoc community groups	1
Business or industry associations	11

[1]Numbers add to more than 26 because of multiple responses

and equity for special and ethnic groups—are problems with which they will have to contend. This does not necessarily mean that groups espousing these points of view will become any more significant as external forces than they are now. The established lever of change and accommodation in all of the participating countries is government; and, in the view of those interviewed, it will continue to be so for the foreseeable future. The likelihood that any of these pressure groups (with the exception of labor unions) will have any direct impact on decision making was viewed as remote by all of those interviewed.

The various countries of Latin America have a general pattern of response which minimizes the importance of pressure groups, maximizes the role of government, and sees the development of the kinds of issues (to the extent that they exist at all) raised by environmentalists, feminist and minority spokesmen, and consumer advocates as being at an embryonic stage. There is still, however, a considerable variety of perceptions among the various Latin American countries where there were study participants. In Argentina, on the one hand, business spokesmen do not see pressure groups or the issues they raise as being of any significance now or in the foreseeable future. In Brazil, on the other hand, most of the issues that are the catalyzing agents for pressure groups have been raised in some way or another—environmentalism, consumerism, even, in one recent instance, feminism. Brazil also has labor unions which are becoming increasingly important, and some church leaders who take strong positions—particularly on labor issues.

Mexico and Chile fall somewhere in between the two extremes of Argentina and Brazil—but lean decidedly more in the direction of Argentina. Mexican unions and industry associations have proven themselves to be active, effective institutions—but, as a general rule, only in pursuing their objectives through government channels.

Finally, there is the question of what each individual means by the word "government." In Mexico, the "government" is the President, and those individuals to whom he delegates authority. Regional and municipal officials, independent regulatory agencies, and court processes are government operations which do not have a significant impact on decison making. "Government" in Mexico means the federal executive branch—pure and simple.

In Argentina and Chile, "government" means the finance ministry—those technocrats to whom the military government has delegated the task of managing the economy. A Chilean case study showed that the government occasionally develops regional responses—especially in university centers where there is a close relationship, cemented by research ties, between the government and the university. No similar kind of regional emphasis was found in Argentina—the government makes determinations solely on the basis of national priorities.

Brazil is the Latin American country which comes closest to the United States and Europe in terms of the airing of issues, the proliferation of pressure groups (albeit with a relatively low profile at this time), and the existence of a federal system with a complex and variegated texture. Brazil, to be sure, has its technocratic finance ministry which, as is the case of Chile and Argentina, sets national priorities and effects policies which have severe impact on the decision-making process. In addition, however, Brazil has a fairly strong regional government system. These governments have a more difficult time than the federal government in ignoring the demands of environmentalists; and, for that matter, any other claims in which a substantial portion of the local population can be mobilized. In addition, Brazil has regulatory agencies which function on the U.S.

Table 5: Comparison of Influence of Government and Nongovernment Outside Groups in Latin America, the United States, and Europe

Region	Government always more important	Government usually more important	Government usually less important	Outsiders always more important
Latin America	19	5	1	1
Europe	16	30	4	0
United States	33	38	0	1

model with a fair degree of independence. For example, one food company executive notes that the food and drug agencies often adopt U.S. standards for allowing a product on the market.

Finally, there is the question of how to deal with government. Is the procedure institutionalized or is it informal? Who in the organization has the responsibility for making these contacts? How is the company structured to handle this most powerful of external forces, whose impact on company decision making is a fact of life in Latin American countries? Interviews with individual business leaders cast light on the differences, as well as the similiarities, between the approaches of companies in the various countries in which data were gathered.

Mexico

All Mexican businessmen who were interviewed agreed that labor unions and the powerful chambers of industry and commerce can play an important role only to the extent of their ability to persuade the Mexican government that the course of action they advocate is not only best for themselves but beneficial to the country. The role of government in Mexican society is central. One chief executive elaborated in detail:

"Our government is very different from what you have in the United States. The government actually listens to people in the United States. I would not call what we have a dictatorship, but it certainly is not a democracy. In the States, the government caters to groups, here it is the other way around—the groups cater to the government, because government has the last say. In Mexico, for all practical purposes, separation of powers does not really exist. The point of pressure is the executive—that branch controls the legislature and the judiciary. In Mexico, one vote counts—the President's. The reason for this is that the executive controls the money—unlike the United States, where the legislature controls at least some of the purse strings. The President is Santa Claus, everyone has to deal with him.

"Government is also the arbiter of last resort. The Confederations of Industry and Commerce have objectives that sometimes are in conflict. Banks want high interest rates, industries want lower rates, but it is the government that decides, and the government they have to try to influence. They do their best; this is not likely to have much effect, the government is very paternalistic."

Another business leader agreed that the government was all-powerful and made some observations as to how the government selects its priorities:

"As a young man, I studied law in the United States. One of the first things I learned was that the Eastern states have a much stricter standard for railroad tort liability than those in the West. The basic reason for this was that the economic and political power of railroads was greater in the West than in the East. In Mexico you see evidence of this general principle at work in the way the government conducts its business. Legislation is not the issue in, for example, the case of environmentalism. We have environmental legislation, but, because the pressure of an aroused public simply does not exist, it is not applied. The government has nothing to gain by enforcement."

This comment illustrates a phenomenon that can be observed throughout Latin America. Governments of all ideological hues often try to establish the environmental and product-safety standards of more advanced industrial nations. However, as the statement demonstrates, implementation and enforcement can be haphazard because the legislation or regulation is "top-down" in character. In short, since the legislation was not passed in response to the demands of an aroused citizenry, there is no constituency to insist that it be enforced.

Discussions with Mexican business leaders indicate that there are two distinct kinds of government pressure which are part of the environment with which Mexican business must contend. In the first instance, government is a party to the contract, and the company must deal with a party with bargaining powers much greater and more arbitrary than its own. While a company has legal remedies, a threatened government cancellation, as an example below will show, often results in renegotiation of a contract. A variant of this model is found in those industries where the government is also active and private enterprise has to compete with a rival that is not subject to the same need for profit margins.

The second kind of governmental activity is the promulgation of governmental policies which are responsive to rival constituencies—invariably labor unions in the case of Mexico. The technique for dealing with both of these problems is preventive at the initial stage—maintain a good network of informal contacts so that these problems are avoided wherever possible. When the preventive approach does not succeed, more formal institutionalized negotiations are the means of resolution. If the problem is specific to the company, the company will present its case directly to the government. If it involves an entire industry (e.g., chemical) one chamber of the Confederation of Industry Chambers which represents the chemical industry will make the presentation. If the issue involves industry as a whole, the entire confederation will meet with the government. If the government's policy affects all business, both the confederations of industry and commerce will act. The latter course has been rare in recent years, but one individual recalled that it was necessary during the term of Luis

Echeverria Alvarez, the president of Mexico from 1970 to 1976.

The Government Contract

One chief executive provided an example of the hazards of doing business with the Mexican government: "We had a contract with the government. The government decided it wanted foreign participation on this deal. The government had a lot of pressure it could use in this situation—granting or withholding of import and manufacturing permits and, as a last resort, cancellation of the contract.

"We had a few things going for us, primarily a potential lawsuit against the government for breach of contract. We worked out a deal. While the government originally wanted half the job for the foreign bidder we whittled it down to one-fourth. We used a lot of high-level technical people in these negotiations—it involved some very technical aspects of the contract—equipment and technical compatibility, for example. If you are going to have two different companies doing the same job, you have to decide which one can best perform each task. We had to work out price differentials, and new delivery times. These issues utilized our top-level sales and technical personnel. I only got in at the very end—for the final negotiations.

"This pressure had some definite effects on the final terms and conditions. Because of the length of time consumed by negotiations, the delivery time was six months late and the price was higher to compensate us for the one-quarter of the contract we lost."

In the view of this individual, operating in this kind of environment requires the "preservation of constant access to government officials, each individual at each level has contacts he must maintain. As far as tactics, what kind of choice is there? The only method is negotiation. It is best, wherever possible, to work through institutional channels—the Confederation of Industrial Chambers. Of course, where the problem is specific to the company, you have to deal directly with the government."

Government Policies

Governmental policies that are responsive to union constituencies are another example of external pressure on Mexican business. One chief executive put it this way: "Price controls are the unions' preferred method to control inflation. It is the best way for their members to maintain the purchasing power of their earnings. In exchange, of course, they tell the government they are willing to moderate their wage demands. The use of price controls in several sectors of consumer products (and their potential implementation in new areas) makes it difficult to make investment decisions in those sectors, because the profit margins simply are not adequate. It has been difficult to convince boards of directors to accept new projects or to increase investment in these areas. Currently, we are considering new products which are affected by controls. A pending decision is not final yet, but we undoubtedly would have gone ahead had the government's price-control policy been different.''

This individual's tactic for dealing with the government differed only slightly in emphasis from that of the executive with the government contract—maintain contacts and negotiate. But he saw a problem in hiring people simply for their government contacts: "We look for good generalists with sound experience, and a good public relations sense, contacts are of secondary importance. After all, the president of Mexico is only in office for six years and we hope to be in business for longer than that.''

Dealing with government, however, requires extreme delicacy: "There is a long tradition of open dialogue between the government and the federations of industry and commerce. A lot gets done through these channels—but it gets done very casuistically, I say casuistically, because although the federation has never denied assistance, if you have a unique case, you really have to negotiate directly, and argue convincingly that your position is justified on moral as well as business grounds.''

Union Organizing

A bank president described the attempt of labor unions to organize the banking industry. "The unions are not attempting to organize individual banks. We have had no direct contact with them. the labor unions are trying to gain representation of all employees in the banking industry through legislation. We do not confront them directly.

"Our approach is low profile and two-pronged. We maintain direct informal contacts at all levels with the public, the government, and our employees. We try to explain to them in a very general way where their real interests lie. We never respond specifically or directly. Sometimes we wait a while, and I'll give a speech which addresses the issue in an indirect manner: We leave it to the listener to make the connection. We do not respond directly to charges. We do it in our own way at a time of our own choosing, but no charge goes unanswered.''

More than others interviewed, this individual emphasized the importance of personal contacts. "The personal element and informality is the critical aspect of our approach. It is reflected at all levels—for me as president of the bank it is important to have contact with everyone. I am on good terms with the President of Mexico, but I think it is equally important to have good relations with my own employees. After all, many of them will be working for the bank after the president leaves office. We have to find a way for everyone at least to have a say; that is why we have an open-door policy for employees.

"I am also in contact with people in the army and the Church. I do not always agree with them, but at least they know that I am available and will listen. We also make geographic as well as industrial representation on the board of directors an important consideration. Because of this approach, I think that, although as time goes on we may have to deal with many of the same problems that currently exist in the United States, our methods will be different. In Mexico the personal element will always be very important.''

Argentina

The view was universal among those interviewed that Argentina is passing through a unique and critical point in her history. Of the business communities in Latin America that participated in the study, none contends with greater external pressure from the government. In spite of this fact, the kind of issues which are the catalytic agents for outside involvement—collective bargaining demands, pollution, women's and minority rights, and consumer safety—are hardly ever raised in Argentina.

One chief executive said: "We Argentines simply do not have a tradition of complaining about problems. Add that tradition, or nontradition if you like, to a lack of representative government and a weak sense of community, and you have a climate in which these issues rarely arise. The whole educational process is geared to an acceptance of hierarchies, so what is the major agent of change in other societies is also lacking. Put these things together and you have circumstances in which people rarely complain. I remember in the neighborhood I used to live in there was this terrible pothole. People used to hit it all the time in their cars; sometimes I would wake up in the middle of the night when people really smacked into that thing. They would get out of their cars and scream and swear, but in all the time I lived in that neighborhood, no one ever complained, and nothing was ever done about it.''

There are two reasons why Argentine business confronts greater governmental impact on decision making than do businesses in the other countries in Latin America that were visited for this study. The first is a situation which is not unusual in Latin America—government participation in key industries. The second is draconian governmental economic policies to combat one of the highest inflation rates in the world. The extensive position of the government in various state-owned enterprises complicates its own anti-inflation efforts and requires companies in the private sector to adapt to both government policies and government competition. With respect to the latter, an executive with a large firm discussed in detail the disparity between the rhetoric and the reality of government involvement in private enterprise:

"Historically, the government is nationalistic and statist. Consistent with this view Argentine governments have felt that all, or at least part, of strategic industries should be in state hands. The result is that many industries are burdened by state competition. The government is the major steel producer, the largest shipbuilder, manages the largest bank, is active in petrochemicals, and in air and water freight. Figures indicate that government-controlled enterprises account for 40 percent of the output of the Argentine economy; I believe that the figure is much higher than that.

"While the rationale for government involvement is strategic and nationalistic, it is also true that government-controlled enterprises have been an extremely good source of employment for retired military officers. This too, has been a problem for us. We had a case some years back where the government stopped a project of ours. Openly the government contended that its reasons were strategic and nationalistic—it did not want us borrowing funds from other countries (which would have been necessary). I think the real motive was to get the project under state supervision in order to obtain the additional employment for some officers who were about to retire. If the whole thing had happened today, I am not sure we would have the same difficulties, but historically this has been a problem in Argentina."

Governmental policies and governmental participation in the economy have had marked effects on company administration. Currently, the policies are of greater concern than the participation. One individual observed that this situation represented an improvement as far as he was concerned: "We have had powerful governmental interference for many years in this country. The government has used two approaches—paternalism and intervention. Recent initiatives have sought to avoid these pitfalls and to take the country into a market economy. Ultimately this will mean less presence of the government in decision making. The kind of interference we had in the past was unpredictable in its occurrence and in its consequences. Today, government pressure on this company is due to two well-established government anti-inflation policies: (1) the opening of the economy to the international market and the acceptance of foreign competition; (2) the current rate of exchange for the Argentine peso."

This individual, an executive with a large holding company, noted that these government policies had resulted in a centralized approach to developing and disseminating an economic model which has, in many instances, a decisive effect on decision making. "We have a decentralized administrative structure, but these government policies require a thorough understanding of the government's objectives and how effectively they are being achieved. First, we develop a macroeconomic model for Argentina. We have opportunities for discussions with the government, so this scenario is developed at the corporate office. We then send it out to the divisions, and to the companies in which we have a major interest. It is up to the managers to interpret and apply the model.

"As far as assembling the information for the model, our managers will discuss technical problems with government officials at various levels. A manager is not required to engage in this kind of activity but many of them have made helpful contributions in this way.

"In this instance, the scenario is just one aspect of a thorough control of company planning. While it is, in large measure, within the manager's discretion as to how to apply the scenario and when to consult corporate headquarters, there are further controls which are the result of company style rather than external pressure: Our style of management is management by objective, and strategic planning. That blueprint determines in large measure whether the corporate office is consulted."

Despite this emphasis on planning and the use of an economic model for all operations, the company remains committed to decentralization, and considers its current approach to be a necessary expedient as a result of external circumstances. The individual manager remains the key: "Once the government model is successful, managers will be able to do what they were trained to do. Our managers have been trained for a market economy which did not exist. The company's problems relate to this difficult transition period. Our people have the technical skill. That has always been important to us, so important that staffing and promotions are among the few centralized functions. To put it bluntly, many companies are good at lobbying, and not at producing or marketing. We think this economic model will give our managers a chance to use their management skills."

Another individual agreed that operational effectiveness and fundamental management skills were critical, especially at the middle levels: "So much of top management's time is devoted to dealing with the government, those middle-level people really have to know how to run the company. Other companies have emphasized governmental relations at all levels, at the expense of operational effectiveness. We think this is shortsighted for two reasons. First, the government changes so often—as soon as you start feeding it, it's gone. Second, sooner or later you have to start operating like a business again. When that day comes we will need all the technical management skills we can get."

The need for an authoritative response externally, and a unified interpretation of governmental policy internally, in the opinion of most executives, leads to greater centralization. One company director differed from this view somewhat: "We are a decentralized organization; each division is organized as though it were a separate company. We delegate decision making in order to have a more flexible response. Externally we do a lot of lobbying, but things happen so fast we have to organize task forces on an ad hoc basis. For these problems we rely on the matrix approach. Someone is put in charge of developing information and making the necessary contacts."

The impact of a chaotic economy which is managed by a highly centralized government has also resulted in heavy emphasis on management information systems and cost controls. Management information systems are critical because of constantly changing government policy. As one executive put it: "We have to have an accounting system which reflects outside factors *immediately,* and we need a good understanding on the part of the entire company as to how this system works."

Management information systems are, of course, critical in achieving cost controls, which are heavily emphasized as a result of the particular policies the government has chosen to combat inflation. From 1979 on, interest rates in Argentina have fluctuated from a real rate of interest of over 100 percent to a real rate of minus 100 percent, depending on the month in question. This has focused attention on the cost side of the ledger. One executive noted: "The only way we can survive is to reduce costs and streamline the company as aggressively as we can. We have reduced our staff by 30 percent and done everything we can to achieve control over energy costs. These are the only approaches left to us. The best solution would be modernization of plant facilities, but that is out of the question right now. The government's current policies discourage investment."

Only one company reported an incident of external pressure of the more conventional sort. In this instance, the government pressured the company to rehire four union leaders. In recalling the episode the company director said: "I think what happened in this case was that the unions put pressure on the Church, and the Church persuaded the government it ought to do something. We argued our case directly to the government, and I think that we prevailed for two reasons. First, these particular individuals had no legal right to be rehired. Second, I do not think the case was particularly important to the government, they were just going through the motions. Still, I think the whole thing may indicate the direction in which the government is going. Unions are going to become more important. Next year there will probably be collective bargaining."

Not surprisingly, all those interviewed said their companies used a low-profile approach in dealing with the government. One individual, however, made a revealing observation as to how a company can present its case to a centralized government which is administered by a technocratic elite: "We have a technical profile. It is neither high nor low. We are not lobbying. We work from general indicators. This, and not industry health, is the basis of our contact with the government."

Brazil

There is much about Brazil that is characteristic of the rest of Latin America with respect to outside forces and their impact on decision making. Government, in the view of those interviewed, is still the primary force with which they have to contend.

If there is much about Brazil that is similar to the other countries which are part of this study, there is also a great deal that is different. While government is still the primary external force, some of the issues raised by government have a great deal in common with those controversies that have arisen in the United States and Western Europe—environmentalism and consumerism.

Brazil has active press and electronic media that serve as vehicles of protest for its fledgling environmental, anti-nuclear and feminist groups. Many (though not all) of the hierarchy of Brazil's Catholic Church are active in raising social issues, and in supporting its union movement with organizational assistance and public advocacy. Unions are also active, and increasingly independent. In 1979, a strike in Sao Paulo idled over 280,000 workers for more than 40 days, and smaller strikes were reported by many of those interviewed. While government is a party to collective bargaining talks, and its unwillingness to approve some of the union demands prolonged the strike, the government is not, as in other Latin American countries, a conduit for union demands. There is direct confrontation between companies and unions and, in some instances, between unions and government.

There is little doubt among those interviewed that all of these processes will continue and become more important and dramatic within the next decade. Brazil's government has announced an "opening to democracy" and appears to be committed to making the political process freer and more participatory. A major initiative in this direction is the encouragement of collective bargaining. Brazil's press and television have a lively interest in industrial scandal, and the threat of exposure and public indignation is always present.

Brazil has a governmental apparatus which enforces product safety and food and drug standards. When asked where the pressure comes for the strict requirements enforced by the latter agency, one individual replied: "There is no pressure from public opinion. The people in charge over there simply feel that no drug which is indexed in the United States by the Food and Drug

Administration should be marketed here. If it is not safe for Americans, it is not safe for Brazilians."

Brazil also has a strong system of regional and local governments, which makes it easier for environmentalists to get action. Two companies reported problems involving environmental issues in San Jose dos Campos. In each case, community groups had persuaded the mayor to discuss changes in practices with the company. It would have been much more difficult to have obtained that kind of attention from a national government because the group would have represented a smaller percentage of its total constituency.

Finally, the multinationals and Brazil's export economy give Brazil exposure to advanced industrial standards in consumer and factory safety. A number of companies that export, or are multinationals, said that these factors contributed in their case to higher standards than would otherwise be required by Brazilian law or commercial practice.

From all this it is evident that Brazilian business must contend with issues and pressures not present in other Latin American countries as a result of Brazil's greater exposure to the outside world. This is particularly true in labor relations. Brazil's labor leaders are quite open about the money and organizational assistance they have received from European unions. In addition, individuals in the Brazilian labor movement have gone to Europe for additional training. Recent bargaining demands reflect this European orientation—some unions, for example, have demanded participation on the shop floor. A group of unions also asked the Industrial Federation for representation on all boards of directors.

While there is little chance of the second demand being realized in the near future, the first has been, or is about to be, achieved in a number of instances. Volkswagen has allowed workers to elect shop stewards, a move the government was willing to approve on the condition that all employees, and not just union members, vote in the election. This, of course, angered the union and its leadership publicly attacked this policy. In the past, other companies have been willing to approve the union election of shop stewards to represent employees in grievances, and to raise issues of general working conditions, but the government, whose approval is essential, has balked.

This seems less likely now, with the "opening to democracy," and some of those interviewed expect to see shop stewards in their companies in the future. As one executive put it, the labor movement is going much further in the European direction, in demanding greater participation, than it is in following the U.S. model of bread-and-butter unionism. Unions are more interested in participation in the management process and broad-based political objectives than in wage packages. Taking a leaf from the labor movement's book, this executive's company—and some of the others interviewed—have

upgraded their labor relations staffs and sent key personnel to Europe for consultation with experienced European labor practitioners.

In spite of these developments, there are enormous regional variations. One executive from Sao Paulo commented: "Sao Paulo is practically a developed country inside of an underdeveloped country. Many of these issues like environmentalism and consumerism do not exist in other parts of the country."

As one might expect from a country with such divergent characteristics, the Brazilian approach to external forces is a hybrid version of the tactics and organization used in South America and those employed in more advanced industrial countries. To begin with, the government, as in all Latin American countries, is still the primary, if not the exclusive, external force with which business has to deal. In certain industries, business must compete with, coexist or do business with government-owned companies.

Despite the existence of the multinationals or, perhaps, because of the need to protect national economic goals against them, the Brazilian government is extremely sensitive to the intrusion of foreign business or capital. As a result, joint ventures, foreign financing, even the importation of component parts, require serious negotiations with the government, while rival concerns are advocating their own version of the "national interest."

In the name of the "national interest," multinationals sometimes argue against further involvement of foreign companies. One Brazilian businessman, who has had great difficulty in importing component parts, lamented: "When it comes to economic nationalism, and the abuses committed in its name, the worst offenders are sometimes the multinationals. Once they get into the country, they complain whenever the Brazilian companies try to get approval for imports, joint ventures, or outside financing. It is as though the last one in tries to close the door behind him."

The national interest also justifies the nationalization of key industries on strategic grounds. One individual, who was fighting off just such a nationalization attempt, and was on his way to Brasilia the following morning to discuss the problem with the government, commented on his experience. "It is not the government, we get along well enough with it. It is all those bureaucrats who think that they can run our industry better than we can."

Thus governmental relations have the highest priority in Brazil, as in the rest of Latin America. Because the location of the Brazilian capital away from the business and financial centers of the nation makes it difficult and expensive to have an office in the capital, only one company interviewed actually had an office in Brasilia. Another company has a branch in Rio de Janeiro (its headquarters are in Sao Paulo) "where most of the social contacts with government officials are." An executive with another company noted: "The president's private jet is used for that purpose, but an office in Brazilia does not make sense."

Even in its dealings with the government, however, Brazilian business shows signs of borrowing American and European tactics. Traditionally the business approach is low profile, as in the rest of Latin America. One company, however, prints its own magazine, which it distributes six times a year to governmental employees. The president of that company noted: "We send these directly to their homes. If you send them to the office, they can get lost." In addition, the company publishes two issues a year in English. These are abstracts of the Portuguese editions.

As to how companies are organized to meet these challenges of external forces, again the uniqueness of the Brazilian situation is an important factor. The relative strength of local government, the environmental issues— as well as the greater power and independence of unions—put more pressure on the plant manager to listen to and accurately report problems to higher level officials within the company. The previously discussed labor unrest in Sao Paulo, and the environmental concerns of the residents of San Jose dos Campos, are cases in point. One company president stated: "Where he can, the plant manager decides. If he cannot, he refers the problem to the proper technical person. If the complaint affects company policy, the board of directors must ultimately approve any initiative or decide what is to be done."

Consistent with the increased power of labor unions, and the interest of the government and the public in environmental and consumer issues, many companies have upgraded staff and/or added additional personnel in these areas. One executive commented bluntly that "The labor relations person used to be second-rate. With the increased power of the unions, and the government's new stance in opening up the political process, we have found it necessary to hire a first-rate person for that position. In addition, other top executives have acquired at least a passing familiarity with labor issues."

Among multinationals, at least in the view of those interviewed, the parent does not get involved in the efforts to handle these kinds of issues. In some cases, the parent may, however, provide seminars on problem solving in sensitive areas. As one president of a Brazilian subsidiary put it: "Our job is to resolve the problem here. We report to the parent, but we are supposed to settle these kinds of matters in this office, and we have been given the authority to do so. The parent is primarily a resource in this regard. Sometimes they have seminars in Brazil, and they also give us access to those kinds of special resources that make it easier for us to decide what to do."

Chapter 5
Japan

JAPAN'S AVOIDANCE of the kind of conflicts that beset the Western industrial democracies has been widely commented upon. These explanations stress the homogeneity of Japanese society, the consensus approach to decision making, and the stoic acceptance by the Japanese of conditions which would provoke protest in Europe or the United States.

While these conditions (and others which will be noted later) may have enabled Japanese industry to function in a remarkably stable and cohesive environment which is the envy of many industrial concerns in other countries, Japanese business must also contend with external forces which have a real and discernible impact on the decision-making process. In this process there is much that will be familiar to the Western business leader and some things that will sound different.

Among the differences—certain avenues such as the courtroom, or the shareholders' meeting, which are useful to American or European groups, are not nearly so helpful to a Japanese counterpart. On the other hand, Japanese tradition requires meetings with groups that have a legitimate grievance to discuss matters of mutual concern. This tradition provides a vehicle for protest which is not generally available to American and European organizations. Moreover, of the various issues and groups under discussion, some (particularly consumer and environmental complaints) are the subject of passionate debate, while others generate little or no support. Japanese concern for consumer and environmental issues, and the relative unimportance of other problems, is best understood by analyzing the nature of the various controversies between business and external forces, and how receptive the Japanese public and Japanese culture are to these various issues.

Regardless of where they occur, most confrontations between business organizations and outside groups in any country can be placed into one of three basic categories: (1) issues of distribution, (2) issues of rights, and (3) issues of corporate responsibility for the side effects of industrialism.

In Japan, the first two categories of protest rarely arise in the private sector. Distributive issues are concerned primarily with the equitable distribution of the company's earnings to its employees. The typical group for airing distributive issues is the labor union.

While Japan has an active labor movement, the overwhelming proportion of union employees belong to a company union. Negotiations are between the company and the leaders of a particular group of company employees. No single union represents all the employees of a given industry. In some cases the union leaders eventually become labor relations executives. In fact, approximately 16 percent of the directors of major corporations are former union officials. This intracompany approach means that distributive issues are generally resolved within the company on a basis of mutual interest and concern in an atmosphere of relative employment security and stability. There are, of course, exceptions to this rule, but they are not widespread. Although this is true in the private sector, in areas of public employment, unions are unusually militant even by Western standards.

The second major area of conflict, the issue of "rights," is also a quiet arena in Japanese industrial society. There are, however, two active "minorities" in Japan—the burakamin (who are the subject of a later case study), and the Koreans. Compared with countries like the United States, activity is limited, but it does exist. Rights of handicapped persons, an area of growing importance in the United States, is more an issue of corporate responsibility than one turning on the inherent rights of handicapped persons.

The remaining "rights" issue—feminism—has a significant and vocal constituency. Although Japan does have an active feminist movement, it is a group which is deprived, in large measure, of issues and the forums in which to exploit them in the industrial context. Few women have reached managerial status in Japan, so that the conflict over equal pay has yet to arouse large numbers of women. Moreover, when women actively pursue these grievances, two vehicles of protest which have been most helpful to women in the United States are less useful to Japanese women.

The first of these avenues is litigation. As a senior executive of one of the largest Japanese companies, who is a lawyer educated in the United States, put it: "Lawyers are not the major force that they are in America. We have over half the population of the United States, and we have only 11,000 lawyers. Litigation is not common in Japan; Japan is not a litigious society." In fact, even by Western standards, the legal process is lengthy and cumbersome; and it is rarely, if ever, the means of achieving final resolution to any dispute of business responsibility. This, of course, is the general rule—feminists and minority groups have used equal employment litigation, particularly against prefectural and national government offices, with some effect.

The second approach, which has sometimes been helpful to women's movements in the United States, is shareholder pressure—or at least the threat of it. This is not a viable tactic for Japanese feminists because, as this same official noted, "90 percent of all directors are 'inside directors'—company employees." Moreover: "There are interlocking ownership interests—large blocks of shares are controlled by other companies in which we, in turn, have a significant level of participation. We deal with one another on the basis of mutual interest and respect."

With these two avenues of limited value, minorities must rely largely on the press and television to make their grievances known. In recent years, the media have been more receptive than in the past to airing these complaints. But the women's movement has thus far enjoyed only limited success in the private sector in consumer issues, and in marginal social areas such as the image of women in advertising.

The third area of protest, however—corporate responsibility for the harmful effects of industrialism—has been an active one. There are important reasons, rooted in Japanese tradition and culture, why this area has been one in which pressure groups have had considerable impact.

The first of these elements is the sense of responsibility which the Japanese acknowledge toward the immediate group of which they are members. This loyalty is built on a foundation of reciprocity—the mutual exchange of privileges and responsibilities. If anything happens to disturb the fragile harmony resulting from this quid pro quo, conflicts are likely to result. For the individual this group identity manifests itself in loyalty to the company, and for the company it takes the form of loyalty to Japanese society at large.

It is most probably for this reason that it is rare for the so-called distributive issues to be raised and aired in a hostile manner. To the Japanese worker, the union is merely a segment of the larger entity to which he or she owes great responsibility. As such, the union has no separate and distinct existence apart from the company.

This sense of group identification can also be observed in those conflicts which do arise. For example, individual consumer complaints are rare in Japan. Instead, grievants form "victims' groups," which then negotiate with the company. The reasons for this are as much practical as cultural—groups have greater credibility and with the shortage of lawyers can achieve greater efficiency and visibility through concerted activity. Companies are extremely sensitive that their image be one of great social responsibility and are, perhaps, more vulnerable to attack by organized groups on this ground than are businesses in other countries.

The second reason for the success of pressure groups in the area of corporate responsibility for harmful effects of industry is the Japanese emphasis on the *importance of consent*. Americans, in trying to express a Japanese approach to problem solving sometimes call this "participative management," which is not quite accurate. What the Japanese company seeks, both inside the firm and in society at large, is a system of "maximum consultation," whereby all sides have an opportunity to express their points of view.[1] Thus, whenever a plant is closed in one location or opened in another, an interminable series of meetings with union and community officials and all affected employees will most likely take place. Though the outcome is not often affected or changed by them, they are considered essential by management to the necessary building of a consensus for an important business decision. In recent years these sessions have provided protest groups with a forum which is not always available in other countries, and has the capacity to generate unfavorable publicity to which business interests are extremely sensitive. Of course, this only refers to those meetings which the company itself elects to hold. The tradition requires, by and large, that the company meet and discuss with "sincerity" almost any issue of responsibility with a duly constituted protest group. This is a burden which is seldom, if ever, imposed on companies in other countries.

In private conversations, executives stress the importance of "sincerity" both on their part and for the opposition. In this context "sincerity" means an honest desire to end a troublesome and divisive dispute, and a real commitment to the overall welfare of society above and beyond recovery for the grievant's individual injury.

[1]Chie Nakane, *Japanese Society*. Hammondsworth, England: Pelican Books (Revised Edition), 1973, p. 140.

Land and geography are also cultural factors which contribute to public sensitivity on issues of harmful industrial practices. Japanese culture (particularly its Shinto origins) is one of great reverence for the land and for environmental balance. This ancient tradition is reinforced by pragmatic considerations of geography. Most of the surface area of Japan is mountainous—unfit for habitation or cultivation. This leaves a very small area (some estimates are as low as 30 percent) for cultivation and settlement. With a population of 115 million and a desire for self-sufficiency in agricultural production, land is a scarce and valuable resource, and conflicting interests must seek accommodation as to how it can best be utilized. In addition, as fish is a major staple in the Japanese diet, fishermen are a group whose views on environmental and ecological issues require a certain amount of accommodation and respect. Taken as a whole, Japanese tradition plus present reality contribute to circumstances where environmental balance is certain to be a central factor in commonplace industrial issues such as plant location and air and water pollution.

There is one controversy that is outside the traditional categories of dispute between business and society which, for historical reasons, is a particularly emotional one in Japan—nuclear power. Japan's energy position is such that business and governmental leaders see little choice as to the necessity for the development of nuclear energy. For the most part, those opposed to nuclear power are not interested in compromise. For this reason, the tradition of "maximum consultation" is not helpful in this area. Proponents and opponents see little evidence of "sincerity" in the opposition. In addition, as there is no single organization which speaks for the entire opposition to nuclear power, a company could reach an accommodation with one group only to see a rival anti-nuclear organization attempt to thwart its objectives. Although the nuclear power issue is more intractable than most of the consumer and environmental controversies, opposition to nuclear power has its origins in these older, more established movements both of which have a longer history of activity than similar organizations in other countries.

The Consumer Movement

Consumer protest is perhaps the oldest continuous vehicle of antiestablishment behavior in Japanese life. To the Japanese it is an all-encompassing term, which is often used to describe environmentalists, feminists and those who oppose nuclear power. One woman, who has been active in the consumer movement for most of her life, said: "I started with consumer activity over 50 years ago when I first got out of University. I was also active in the trade union and feminist movement at that time. A lot of things have happened since then, but government and big business are still very powerful and sometimes

they operate together. We have had continuous disappointments, but we have to keep on fighting. Still, there is reason for encouragement. The interest of the public is increasing, and we now have scholars and professionals involved in our activities."

In this woman's view, the consumer movement has five "main currents," ranging from semiofficial government organizations to ad hoc "grass root" groups. Although these five different types have distinct spheres of activity, they do combine their resources on some issues. Two of these organizations are at least nominally women's, or "housewives," organizations.

Shufuren (full name—Shufurengokai—the Japanese Housewives' Association) was founded in 1948. The precipitating cause was the widespread distribution of matches which would not light. Mrs. Mumeo Oku, a member of the Japanese Diet's Upper House, called for a "Mass Meeting to Collect Non-lighting Matches" in Tokyo, and that really was the beginning of what many consumer activists regard as the senior organization of the consumer movement.

In 1956, Shufuren established the Shufukaikan (Housewives' Hall), which has facilities for testing consumer goods such as food and clothing. One of Shufuren's early successes was the detection of dangerous substances in baby foods. Shufuren is still active in food-substance issues and was instrumental in the passage of a Fair Products Labeling Law. In recent years Shufuren has also focused on the high prices of home-heating kerosene and the nuclear power issue. As of mid-1979, Shufuren had 445 member organizations and was publishing Shufuren Dayori (Shufuren News) as well as pamphlets and research reports on specific issues.

A second woman's organization, the National Federation of Regional Women's Organizations (Chifuren) was founded in 1952. Chifuren has as its primary objective the betterment of the status and welfare of women, but in recent years has become involved in consumer issues as well.

Chifuren's consumer activities have focused in large measure on consumer pricing. One of its successes was the exposure of a discrepancy between the manufacturer's net price for color television sets and the actual selling price. Acting in concert with other women's organizations, Chifuren organized a consumer boycott. The result was a reduction in price of the boycotted items.

Chifuren is also concerned about the high cost of cosmetics in Japan. To combat this problem, Chifuren has produced its own "100-yen cosmetics" manufactured under the name "Chifuren." Chifuren has 51 local organizations and a total membership of 6.5 million.

The Consumers Union of Japan (Nihon Shohisha Remmei) is of more recent origin (1969) and takes a more militant approach to consumer issues. Founded by a former government official, Naokazu Takeuchi, this organization has relied primarily on exposé tactics to denounce deceptive products, services and advertising.

One of the organization's earliest successes was an attack on the door-to-door sales techniques of encyclopedia salesmen. This campaign contributed to the passage of a "Door to Door Sales Law" and to the revision of Japan's Installment Sales Law. More recently, CUJ has been involved in activities to ban synthetic detergents, to improve the safety of cosmetic products, and to eliminate harmful additives and preservatives from processed foods. CUJ is especially interested in encouraging regional grass-roots movements, and it has devoted substantial effort to serving as a bridge between other protest groups—such as environmentalists and antinuclear activists—and the consumer movement.

Grass-roots organizations are the fourth type of consumer group in Japan. Grass-roots organizations vary tremendously in size and description, but they do have a few characteristics in common. To begin with, they are often ad hoc—arising in response to a particular grievance. Sometimes these organizations will also be called "victims' groups." In the case of "victims' groups," participants or members of their family have sustained an injury as a result of the harmful product. Both grass-roots and "victims' groups" have enjoyed considerable success in recent years, particularly in cases involving harmful food and drugs.

More recently, grass-roots movements that have been active in seeking a ban on synthetic detergents, along with CUJ and Shuferen, formed the Liaison Conference of Consumer Groups. This umbrella organization has, on occasion, acted as a single body on certain issues. One of the Conference's more notable victories was the banning of the preservative AF2 on the grounds that it causes cell mutation and is suspected of being carcinogenic.

The fifth element in the Japanese consumer movement is the government, which has two semiofficial organizations—the Japanese Consumers' Association and the National Consumers Information Center. Both of these organizations are devoted to similar activities—the testing of consumer products and the processing of complaints. The Consumers' Association also has a training course for consumer consultants.

The Consumers' Association, however, is not the only government-sponsored organization to provide training on consumer subjects. By some count, there are 2,000 consumer schools in Japan. While these schools are independent, much of their financing comes, directly or indirectly, from the government. Local consumer schools are joined at the national level by the National Consumer Schools Liaison Council.

In late 1980 and early 1981, the government authorized an independent agency to administer a test that will license those who pass as "consumer advocates." A spokesman for one of the more militant consumer organizations said: "Most of these people will go to work for companies and, for this reason, the private consumer organizations have no interest in this process."

This observation is supported by an examination of the mix of applicants and the nature of the test questions. Roughly half of the 2,200 applicants were company employees. It is anticipated that a far larger proportion of those who pass will come from this group. Moreover, the examination consists primarily of hypothetical questions which require the applicant to say how he or she would deal with a consumer complaint as a company official.

In making this licensing procedure available, the government is responding to an increasing need on the part of Japanese business. According to one consumer activist, various companies have established over 500 consumer sections, and the employees in this field have established an Association of Consumer Affairs Professionals. This organization has conferences at which consumer activists are invited to speak. One of the invitees commented: "I think this group is a wolf in sheep's clothing, but we shall have to see." Still, the same individual conceded that the relationship betwen her organization and most consumer divisions is a good one: "We have good communications with consumer sections. The problem is with access to decision makers, and the consumer relations head also has that problem. In America, Nader has struggled with the front office while we are still struggling with the lower levels, and these consumer people can only operate on a case-by-case basis. They cannot make big policy decisions, only the president can do that."

Environmentalists

Compared with the consumer movement, environmentalism is still in its infancy. There is, of course, a tendency in Japan for environmentalism and consumerism to be somewhat synonymous. The more militant consumer organizations are actively involved in environmentalism and consider all their targets to be industrial hazards.

Environmentalism is also an active area for those movements that favor a return to traditional ways with an emphasis on a more rural society, greater reverence for the land, and harmony with nature. Fishing and agricultural groups also pursue environmental objectives, largely out of self-interest.

If a contrast could be found between the environmental and the consumer movements in Japan, it is that environmentalists are organized primarily in local, ad hoc groups. Secondly, the environmentalists tend to be more militant than the consumer advocates. Sit-ins and direct confrontations are not uncommon on environmental issues.

One leader of the environmental movement commented: "I do not know the exact number of environmental groups. Back in 1972 or 1973, the police considered us something of a security problem and said there were about 3,000 environmental groups, I think there are only around 1,000."

This particular activist also saw the environmental movement as having more broad-based political objectives than merely achieving a particular result in a specific confrontation:

"In the rural areas our movement is largely lower-middle class. There is more regard for nature in those parts of the country, and, of course, farmers and fishermen are concerned about these problems. It is all part of a movement for self-education and greater independence from central authority. I also think that the environmental battle is a feminist movement, but not in the Western sense—it is a movement of women, but not a women's movement. If the power of women is strong, then we are stronger. Women are more active, less willing to compromise. Where we have been successful, women have always been in the majority. In the cities, of course, it is more of a middle-class operation because everyone is middle class to begin with."

In general, environmentalists seek, often by confrontation, to influence the climate of opinion not just on the particular issues of the moment, but also on the direction of Japanese culture and society. This approach, along with the ponderous nature of the Japanese judicial system, relegates the courtroom to a less important position than it occupies in other countries. As one individual noted: "The role of the court is to define liability. This can be a factor in negotiations, and can influence public opinion, but the verdict is not the end—it is just the beginning—then the hard bargaining begins."

External Forces: General Observations

The specific conflicts between Japanese companies and pressure groups (which will be discussed in detail) lend themselves to certain generalizations at the outset.

First, nearly all of the confrontations observed are concerned with consumer or environmental issues. There is little evidence of protest involving issues such as feminism, investment policy, or wages, hours and working conditions. Isolated examples exist of problems involving plant relocation, minority hiring practices, and governmental relations. These will be discussed, but they are not commonplace, and they are not among the day-to-day concerns of the Japanese companies. Consumer and environmental (and this includes nuclear power) problems are clearly of interest to the Japanese public and exposure of bad practices in the these areas can (and has) aroused large constituencies.

Secondly, these case studies show the ad hoc nature of

the group exerting the pressure. While there are a few national organizations (particularly in the consumer area) that are engaged in continuous activity on a variety of issues, these organizations are rarely involved directly with companies.

The pattern is for a group of grievants to approach a national organization and to ask for guidance as to how to deal with the company. As one consumer advocate put it: "If a group comes to us with a complaint, we tell them to form a 'victims' group,' hire a lawyer, and take action by themselves."

In large measure, the national organizations, if they are involved at all, exist to give advice on techniques of dealing with the company, to provide expert witnesses for trials, to do research on a product's harmful effects, and to lobby at the national level with Diet members and officials of various ministries. Corporate executives deal almost exclusively with those who are *directly* affected by company actions. Even in cases where the impact is nationwide, such as a dangerous drug, the so-called "victims' group" will be divided into separate organizations by prefecture, and the company must deal with each one of these groups on an individual basis.

The key, however, remains the group nature of the protest. Individual grievants are rare in Japan—single persons do not often sue companies or denounce them for harmful practices. Although it is theoretically possible for an individual to pursue a complaint, it rarely happens—preference for group activity rests on the view that group effort is still the most effective means for achieving a settlement.

Third, while the legal process is an integral part of a campaign, it does not play the important role that it occupies in other countries. When the courtroom is employed it is used to expose, to marshal support, and to determine liability. Once this has been done, both the company and the group will begin bargaining in earnest and both sides will be attentive to the views of support and opposition that the trial has generated. As in other countries, a court case often leads to a rethinking of the company position with respect to outside contacts. Like it or not, one of these "contacts" is usually the government. It is not unusual, for example, for the government to exert pressure on a company to settle once a trial court has determined that liability exists. This, of course, would be considered a wholly unwarranted intrusion in the legal process in many countries. It occurs in Japan for three reasons: (1) the government is often a codefendant and does not want its own activities to be exposed to close scrutiny; (2) the government has a special interest in the good reputation of the country's business practices; and (3) the government is accepted by the parties as a mediator. It should be remembered, of course, that the government is not a monolith—sometimes a company will find itself caught in the cross fire between ministries which have opposing views on a given issue.

Consistent with the general difficulty of reconciling protest with legal concepts is the difficulty that Japanese companies have in understanding the concept of strict liability. In Japan, the sense of individual responsibility is very strong, and where a company's practices are proven to be a proximate cause of injuries, organizations (and even individuals who may not have been personally at fault) will acknowledge error readily. Where, however, another company in the chain of distribution is culpable, or there is no clear causal relationship between their activities and the injury, or a government agency has given its imprimatur to a harmful product, it is difficult to get a company to compensate victims. Such compensation would be an admission of bad conduct which did not occur and not, as it is in other countries, one of the costs of business which must be acknowledged, particularly when dealing with potentially hazardous products, or when employing hazardous methods.

Fourth, the emphasis by all parties on the importance of "sincerity" is a critical element in dispute resolution. "Sincerity" means more in this context than the English meaning of "honest," "genuine" or "real." To the Japanese it entails a patient willingness to listen to all sides, an openness to another point of view, an acknowledgment that the other side is acting in good faith, and a willingness to take its views into consideration. "Sincerity" involves the inclusion of an adversary in the Japanese system of "maximum consultation." In short, one must listen seriously to "sincere" persons, even if the company has already decided on a course of action.

Is the concept of "sincerity" really more than a prescription for an elaborate minuet? The answer is yes and no. While business decisions are rarely changed or modified as the result of negotiation between "sincere" parties, they sometimes are, and this kind of meeting implies conditional acceptance which may lead to collaboration and prior consultation on future ventures in which the previously hostile group really will have its views taken into account. In any event, the issue is not how much change has occurred but, rather, the conditional acceptance of one another by the parties. The process is far more important than the outcome. Moreover, parties that are not viewed as "sincere" are ignored altogether. When ignored in this manner, some groups will employ more hostile and confrontational methods such as sit-ins, and violence may occur in some instances.

Fifth, the Japanese style decision-making "ringi" of obtaining some sort of consensus inside the company is rarely employed in managing this kind of conflict. There is a need for a quick response and thus decisions are usually made after consultation between the consumer department, the executive vice president for administration, and the manager in charge of the product or area involved.

Moreover, in issues of accepting liability, or allocating it between firms that may be jointly liable, the decision is made by the chief executive with little or no consultation at lower levels. If the issue is one of determining the relative liability as between two companies, the chief executives of the two organizations will negotiate between themselves as to the degree of economic exposure each organization will accept.

Sixth, the press is a major factor in these disputes as it is in most countries, but it must be handled differently. Japanese reporters are organized into "press clubs," which include all the journalists from major papers and networks covering a particular activity. Many contacts between companies and the press are channeled through this semiformal institution. The "press club" is determined that all its members have equal access, indeed its ability to make good on that guarantee is one of its prime reasons for existing. In addition, reporters rotate in given assignments every two years—this short period means that on many issues companies must deal with inexperienced reporters and in a group. Companies can invite individual reporters for a briefing—but only those who are not members of "press clubs." Companies have explored alternatives to this approach, but this institution makes it difficult for a company to advocate its position strongly unless it wishes to do so in all major newspapers and networks.

CHEMICAL COMPANY A—Adjusting to Changing Concepts of Liability: A Hardline Response

A chemical company's struggles with the single cell protein issue is illustrative of many of the basic characteristics of conflicts between companies and pressure groups in Japan. The company is a medium-sized manufacturer of chemical products, which also produces foodstuffs. Among the foodstuffs, edible oil and related products are the major sales items.

The Single Cell Protein Issue

Single cell protein (SCP) was a product that the company, along with other chemical firms, planned to market as a substitute for animal feed. In the early 1970's, after two years of testing, the companies submitted the testing data to the Ministry of Agriculture for authorization. After some delay, the approval was granted. Before production plans could be implemented, the project was embroiled in controversy.

Prodded by Shufuren (the housewives' federation) and various ad hoc groups of academics, the media—which referred to SCP as "naphtha protein"—raised the issue of whether the substance would cause cancer if consumed by humans. Also instrumental in this attack were some of the country's "social critics."

The "social critic" is an influential Japanese institution. While the "social critics" reach their audiences through the usual medium of television or the press, they are somewhat different from the ordinary American investigative reporter. The viewpoints of the "social critics" are likely to be couched in Olympian tones, their stories are longer than the typical newspaper report, and they incorporate additional material about the general nature and direction of Japanese society.

Shufuren, the ad hoc academic groups, and the "social critics" demanded that the government revoke its order authorizing production and sale, and that it restrict the exporting of SCP technology overseas. The attempt to restrict exports was indicative of a major change in perspective of the Japanese consumer movement. As one of its leading advocates put it: "We have to become more interested in the world consumer movement—and not just the United States—Asia is especially important. We think the Japanese are still very isolated. We are concerned that even when we stop something, Japanese business will dump it abroad. Sometimes the use is stopped, but the production is not. That is why we need a world perspective."

Faced with this type of opposition, company officers (including the president and several executives and staff of the research and development department) gave the press information about SCP, including its chemical composition and production methods, but this campaign made little headway. Despite this accessibility, the company was reluctant to confront its critics directly, limiting this type of response to a single appearance on television in which a representative of the company participated in a television discussion on the issue. One executive lamented: "There was no one to talk to. The critics did not understand the technical issues, and they accepted test results only if they confirmed their position."

The controversy eventually reached the political arena. All but one of the opposition parties acted in concert to bring the issue to the Diet and to challenge the government with neglect of public health and safety. The one party which refused to participate in this effort was the Japanese Communist Party, whose spokesman expressed unease at the "unscientific nature of the public debate." This was surprising because the Party is usually supportive of consumer activism, particularly when, as here, it is initiated by Shuferen.

Bowing to this pressure, the government suspended the production authorization pending further testing. In addition, the Ministry of Trade prohibited any export of SCP technology. Despite these setbacks, the company's research and development department still has a small team monitoring SCP developments. Efforts to get on with production are not now aggressive as the company does not want to alienate the public while other litigation involving harmful chemicals is in progress.

Organizational Changes

This experience has had a limited organizational impact on the company. A number of executives conceded that the case was not handled very effectively, and that the company needed more general preparation for incidents of this type. Accordingly, the company has taken the unusual step of establishing a legal department. With the exception of banks and insurance companies, legal offices are a rarity in Japanese companies, although most organizations will have a few legal specialists attached to the president's office.

In this instance, the legal department consists of five individuals, who report to the head of the general affairs department and he, in turn, reports to the president. Thus far this group has had an "informal" effect on the setting of priorities, and on decision making in general. As one individual put it: "We try to go slower and make sure the bases are covered." In addition, the company has increased its public relations activities. All in all, company officials feel that these two measures make the company better equipped to handle future problems that may arise.

CHEMICAL COMPANY B—Conciliation and How It Works

Company B, founded by a merger of two medium-sized chemical firms before World War II, is now one of the leading chemical manufacturers in Japan, with major involvement in plastics, industrial chemicals, and fertilizers. In addition, it has subsidiaries and affiliates, most of which are manufacturers or fabricators of chemical process products.

As was the case with Company A, Company B was involved in a chemical pollution case. Unlike A, the case resulted in fairly substantial changes in the company's approach to the public.

When the case arose, the company's procedure was for the defense effort to be coordinated by the General Affairs department, a staff unit dealing with public affairs activities and attached to the company's main office. This department supervised the team of lawyers retained to represent the company in court.

Coordinating a legal defense in this manner can be difficult because of the fairly low estate of general affairs departments in Japanese companies. As one individual, who is knowledgeable about Japanese corporate life, put it: "An assignment to general affairs as staff is a dead-end proposition. If you are made head of the department, it is a nice reward for services rendered, but you will not go anywhere from there. General Affairs is only important in those few instances where personnel is part of its jurisdiction." The weakness of General Affairs, plus the scarcity of persons near the top with legal training, resulted in a situation where few, if any, persons with decision-making responsibility were fully informed on legal issues.

Still, unlike Company A, Chemical Company B made fairly substantial efforts to settle the case out of court, but these early endeavors were unsuccessful. One executive involved in these negotiations explained why, in his view, these attempts had failed: "I think the plaintiff's lawyers were more interested in achieving the objectives of the radical political organizations with which they were affiliated than in getting a settlement for their clients."

While informal negotiations were breaking down, the company's case was weakened by a government report, concurring with a previous investigation that had identified the company as the most likely source of the chemical contamination. To compound the company's woes, two similar cases of industrial pollution were decided in favor of the plaintiffs while this one was pending. In view of these unfavorable circumstances the company announced, two days prior to the court's decision, that—win or lose—it would accept the verdict of the court and would not appeal.

This decision was not unanimous. As one executive put it: "We all knew that we were going to lose. The president and the board of directors wanted to accept the verdict, but the General Affairs department and the outside lawyers wanted to go ahead with the appeal."

Key executives suggested several reasons for this decision. First, it was believed that a continuation of the legal battle would undermine the morale of the employees who expected their company to play a socially responsible role. These executives pointed to another pollution case where management had decided in favor of a non-conciliatory posture. The result was physical clashes between company employees and the crippled victims of chemical pollution, work stoppages, and a drop in productivity. As the director of corporate planning observed: "The employees have to feel they work in a company they can be proud of." Indeed, this philosophy was advocated by the president, who was a leader of several business organizations, and who saw this as an affirmation of policies he had promoted in the past.

In addition, several members of the board felt that, given the sensitivity of the Japanese public on the pollution issue, the company's chances of prevailing were slim, and that damage to the company's image by continued resistance would far outweigh any potential benefits. It was felt that a prompt payment to needy victims might help to recover lost prestige, and demonstrate the firm's commitment to operate in a manner consistent with the goals of Japanese society. In fact, the decision not to appeal became an integral part of the company's self-promotion effort, which is outlined to new employees in speeches of top executives.

A leading environmental activist, who was involved in the case on behalf of the plaintiffs, had his own view on why the company did not appeal. "Certainly they were concerned about their reputation and pressure from the mass media. But I think it was most helpful to our side that a well-known lawyer said he would pressure the Tokyo government to withdraw all money on deposit with banks that did business with the company."

Organizational Impact

The chemical pollution episode had serious organizational consequences for a company whose leadership attached great importance to community relations. To begin with, the company established a new department to monitor the company's involvement with potentially hazardous products and technologies.

The plant which had been identified by government experts as the source of contamination was shut down; where a similar process was used in other facilities, it was gradually replaced by alternative technologies. One executive observed: "At first these new procedures are bound to affect the speed and scope of technological development in our firm, but I expect this negative effect will last only a short time."

The company also initiated a new set of guidelines for relations with communities surrounding company plants that call for increased participation by residents in monitoring the company's adherence to established pollution norms and standards. For example, in its largest petrochemical complex, the company installed pollution-monitoring devices both inside and outside the plant. The outside devices are checked regularly by a group of volunteers who have no ties to the company. If a problem occurs, these community participants call the plant's operating center on a special telephone line. The company urges them to do so even if the source of pollution is not in the company's facility. Periodically, these residents are invited inside the plant for explanations of plant operations and discussions of pollution-prevention methods.

In addition to the communitywide program of pollution control, the company also initiated a series of excursions by local school children, and has opened most of the company's recreational facilities to residents who are not employees. As a result of these policies, executives feel that the company is "trusted" by local residents and any issues can be settled in a matter-of-fact way, based on a technical analysis of the facts and not on emotions. One of the executives currently involved in negotiating the company's plans for expansion with local government representatives commented: "These programs have been very helpful. Our negotiations are smoother than is usually the case in Japan."

Limits To Cooperation

As one executive noted: "We think we have pretty good community relations, but there are limits. Right now we are having difficulty getting permission to transport poisonous material from one location to another for further processing."

As is the case with many sensitive issues in Japan, the plant manager is a key figure in this problem. (Plant managers are very important company officials and many of them sit on the board of directors.) The plant manager coordinates this effort with managers in charge of technical development, environmental protection, and corporate planning. Although the board of directors does not get involved in individual problems, it does set guidelines as to how various types of issues should be handled. These operating executives also get advice from the public relations and legal sections of the General Affairs Department. The legal section was established as a result of this incident.

Looking to the future, many company executives see environmental issues as only an "intermediate" problem. As one executive noted: "Our concern for the future is primarily with the impact of the crude-oil price explosion. We buy our crude directly from the Middle East and we use it as a raw material for most of our products, which are then sold to other manufacturers for final reprocessing. As the importer, we are concerned about the consumer criticism that has been directed at the oil companies. A special problem for us would be the oil price controls that some of these groups advocate."

Indeed, consumer advocates are concerned about what they call "oil profiteering." Following the 1975 oil crisis, 343 consumer plaintiffs sued the companies for damages suffered by consumers from oil and kerosene "profiteering." The case is still in litigation.

As it is in other matters, the company's approach is to engage in "discussion" with its critics with the hope of explaining that it has no control over OPEC pricing policies; but it is skeptical about the prospect of reaching an understanding. At this point, however, there is no institutional channel of communication with consumer groups. The company's primary focus is its manufacturer customers. Thus, dialogue with the public on this issue is limited to routine public relations activities and occasional appearances by the chief executive.

CHEMICAL COMPANY C—A Problem in Plant Location

Like Company B, one of Company's C's problems arose from alleged chemical poisoning. Unlike Company B, litigation was not involved, and the dispute was resolved in a more traditional Japanese manner.

The company is a leading manufacturer of diversified chemical products. Its main product lines are various industrial chemicals, fertilizers, plastics and, more recently, pharmaceuticals. The company belongs to one of the largest industrial groups in Japan. The top management of the company is very stable compared with others in the industry; the current chairman has served as a de facto chief operating officer for more than two decades. The firm has manufacturing facilities on all four Japanese islands.

In the opinion of one of its directors, plant location is a major headache for the company. The problem is that the plants (especially those established before the war) are too close to residential areas. In addition, many of these plants were constructed on the shore to facilitate delivery of incoming raw materials and removal of finished products by ships. As many of the early industrial pollution cases involved water-pollution issues, the Japanese public is sensitive to the problems of coastal locations for chemical plants. Among the most active constituencies in resisting attempts by chemical companies to locate plants in coastal areas are the fishermen's cooperatives. These groups fear that their customers are less likely to purchase fish caught in coastal waters near chemical plants.

In one particular episode, the local fishermen's cooperative demanded compensation for damages it alleged were suffered by its members as the result of pollution from the industrial waste from one of the plants. The incident may well have been prompted by press coverage of several mercury poisoning cases. The fishermen had little difficulty in gaining the company's attention. They published a list of demands and obstructed the sea access to the plant with their fishing boats. At one point, the fishermen also obstructed the plant's sewer system outlet with sandbags. As a result of these actions, the plant was forced to suspend operations.

The company was never in doubt as to its liability. It used a "closed system" technology in which potentially harmful chemicals were recycled and never actually released outside the plant. In its view, therefore, the fishermen never suffered any actual damages. The company was nevertheless willing to negotiate with representatives of the cooperatives (who had managed to gain some support from local government officials) to compensate them for "spiritual damages" resulting from fear of mercury poisoning. The plant manager (who was also a director of the firm) represented the company in this undertaking, and he consulted with other executives at corporate headquarters. The final decision was approved by the board of directors without much debate.

The incident surprised the company because the fishermen's case was a weak one: "The plant was relatively new; it had advanced antipollution equipment, and it was relatively far (over one kilometer) from the community. Clearly, the fishermen's protest had its roots in an issue of a more general nature—the overindustrialization of the region during the previous decade. One notable manifestation of this growth was the steel mill (one of the largest to come on stream in Japan in the middle 1960's) on land that was previously used for agriculture. Prior to this episode, the company had not had much interest in issues of this sort. As a result of this experience, each plant manager is now responsible for full-scale monitoring of local attitudes.

Organizational Response

Reacting to the heightened concerns of local residents which resulted from the fishermen's protest, the company discontinued the controversial manufacturing process. In fact, conversion of the plant discussed in this case took place before the company received any instructions from the Trade Ministry. The company also began consulting with local government groups to explain their manufacturing procedures. These meetings have achieved varying degrees of success, but company officials feel that relationships with local governments are much more harmonious than they were in the early 1970's.

In order to maintain the current state of cooperation, the company has instituted some early warning systems which will help it to be sensitive to developing issues and will give it the capacity to respond quickly on urgent issues. To achieve these objectives the composition of the "pollution control committee" was upgraded. One of the senior managing directors (who is a de facto vice-president and chief technical officer) is its chairman. The committee is now composed of 20 people, 12 of them with director or general manager ranking. The membership includes representatives of various plants, and technical staff from the head office, and managers from the finance and planning departments. This gives the committee the capacity to arrive at decisions from a fairly general perspective.

The company has also strengthened the environmental protection section of the corporate technical staff. This section recommends the purchase of various types of "pollution-free" processes, and organizes "environmental inspections" at each of the company's plants. The inspection is conducted by a ten-person team of employees who do not work at the plant, and the group leader is usually one of the company's senior managing directors. The team inspects all aspects of the plan's operations that might have an impact on environmental quality. If problems are discovered, the team and the plant manager work on methods to eliminate them.

Although substantive programs to achieve clean and safe technology are a necessary condition in achieving cooperative relations with local communities, one of the company directors observed that the oft-used word "sincerity" is still the key: "I think 'sincerity' is still most important. By 'sincerity' I mean the company's willingness to listen to complaints of residents; our patience in explaining our position and the technical aspects of our business; and our willingness to compromise, even if the law does not require us to do so."

The company feels that it is important to demonstrate this kind of openness to community viewpoints. Although the president and senior managing directors meet with local prefectural and political leadership, the basic focus is on ties at as many levels as possible. Thus, as in many other Japanese firms, the company encourages plant visits by local residents and school children, and its recreational facilities are open to anyone living near its plants. The company expects that its union will cooperate with management in improving community relations. Although internal publications urge the employees to engage in this kind of activity, the company has yet to devise formal programs instructing workers as to how to represent the firm.

PUBLIC UTILITY COMPANY D—Relations with Consumer Groups and Individuals Who Use their Techniques

Public utilities in all countries are among the major targets of consumer and environmental activists. Japan is no exception to this rule. In the wake of the energy crisis, issues such as rate increases and nuclear power have become more troublesome, while more traditional disputes—such as land conversion for additional power installations—continue to be difficult to resolve.

In their relations with power companies many Japanese consumer groups have established two key objectives: "The recapture of foreign-exchange profits for consumers," and a "nuclear moratorium." The first of these goals—"the recapture of foreign-exchange profits" materialized when the yen appreciated against the dollar during the period 1977-1979. When this occurred, consumer groups charged that electric power and gas companies, big users of imported oil, made enormous profits as a result of the cheaper cost of raw materials. According to one consumer advocate, a broad-based coalition of consumer organizations was successful in getting eight electric power and three city gas companies to reduce their rates in September, 1978.

Nuclear power is a far more complex issue for both the companies and their opposition to handle. Unlike a rate-reduction campaign, there is no single program behind which the opposition can unite. As a result, companies are faced with a broad range of organizations demanding everything from the dismantling of existing facilities to a stricter, more dependable safety program. Some groups will not even negotiate; others are willing to, but no one can be entirely certain of which groups can bind their adherents to any settlement that might be reached with the company.

Thus, any organization's assessment of the objectives of the anti-nuclear movement is risky. Still, a good starting point is probably the program of the Tokyo Local Consumer Organization's Liaison Council and the League of Women Voters:

(1) To shut down all nuclear reactors in Japan and conduct a complete inspection. Furthermore, to immediately disclose to the public accurate information about the actual state of each licensed reactor, without concealing data.

(2) To stop the construction of nuclear reactors from now until their safety is confirmed.

(3) To reform the energy development policy that has been centered on nuclear power, and hasten research, development and application of less polluting technology such as solar energy and thermal energy.

(4) To promote change away from an energy-intensive industrial structure, and to show more concrete measures for energy conservation to the public.

Handling these kinds of issues has been of increasing concern to Company D, one of the largest of Japan's nine electric power utility companies. As a public utility, located in a key metropolitan area, the company must grapple daily with issues raised by rate adjustments, atomic power-plant operations, and high-voltage transmission line construction.

Rate Adjustments

Consumer group involvement in rate adjustments is a comparatively recent phenomenon, dating from the oil crisis of late 1973. Until then, electric power rates were relatively stable, and Japanese consumer groups paid little attention to them. In 1974, however, the company proposed to pass along its higher energy costs to the consumer with a rate hike of nearly 100 percent. In doing so, the company adhered to the procedures it had followed in the past when requesting a single-digit increase. It made no preliminary contacts with consumer organizations, or with the representatives of local government in the areas that were affected. As one executive put it: "We did not know whom to talk to. This had never happened before. There was no precedent; no rules of the game."

This period is now referred to by activists as the "consumer goods panic of 1973," and public utilities were not the only organizations under attack. Responding to actions by several large oil companies, the Fair Trade Commission filed a criminal indictment against the companies accusing them of secret price fixing and a violation of the Anti-Monopoly Law. Following on the heels of this government action, many consumer organizations, led by Shufuren, instituted a class action suit (the first instance of consumer class actions in Japan) against the companies.

It was in this environment that the company announced its planned rate hikes. This notice was greeted by attacks from the newspapers. Television stations (which in many instances are owned by the newspapers) followed their customary practice of reporting the news that appeared in the papers. Consumer groups and local offices of national union federations called for demonstrations and meetings to protest the company's proposal. Looking back on the whole episode, company executives regard it as "eccentrically political" in that there was no real attempt to establish communication on either side. After some delay, the government authorized the company's rate application (and similar requests by other public utilities). Although only minor adjustments had been made to mollify the critics, the company felt that its "corporate image" had suffered considerably.

Organizational Consequences

Anticipating that similar situations might occur in the future, the company took steps to assure greater cooperation or, at least, acquiescence from consumer groups and local governments. Within the marketing division, it established a special department for "rate-making" planning. This department, along with the division's general planning section and public relations office, would coordinate company strategy in the event of future rate hikes. In 1978, after a second rate increase controversy, the company established a "Consumer Consulting Office" to strengthen direct ties to resident consumers. This office was incorporated into the marketing division, and the division's general manager became a managing director.

The company's approach in opening communications with its opposition was two-pronged: "It emphasized increased contact with organized consumers and residents at one level, and improved relations with "grass-roots" activists on the other. Through regular dialogue, it hoped to get across its views over a period of time in a less emotionally charged atmosphere than rate-increase talks. To further this end, the company disseminated a wide range of position papers on various issues related to the price of electricity and invited consumer activists to come and present their comments. Since many of the staff members in consumer organizations (particularly the more established ones like Shufuren and Chifuren) are full-time professionals working on a single issue, the company viewed them as people who could be helpful. As one executive commented: "They have people over there who work full time on a single issue and have developed some expertise. Over time you get to know them, and we can talk to them."

Today when requests for rate-hikes are announced, the company, in concert with metropolitan and prefectural governments and consumer groups, will convene a series of "explanatory meetings" (voluntary public hearings). Top executives (including the president) will present the company's case and respond to audience questions.

These meetings are widely covered by the media, particularly local television stations. Television coverage frequently depicts angry protestors demonstrating against the company's proposed rate increase and executives are reconciled to the need for this "ceremony" in order to achieve smooth passage through the Ministry of Trade hearings which must precede a decision by a special government commission. As the company anticipates a slash in its requests in the final authorization, it asks for a greater increase than it needs.

Company executives are satisfied that the current approach works well. Still, they expect increased opposition and activism from the labor federations. To blunt this expected pressure, the company plans to step up direct communication on pricing issues with customers through direct mail and home visits. Active support of new kinds of company public relations campaigns by employees is strongly encouraged; and for managers, it is expected.

Nuclear Power

Opposition to nuclear power in Japan is, perhaps, as broad-based and well-organized as anywhere else in the world. The anti-nuclear movement has attracted many professionals with the technical expertise to dispute any claim which a company might advance. Anti-nuclear forces have also received support from several opposition political parties. Not all of these various opposition forces are even interested in negotiating with the power companies; for some, the objective is an end to nuclear power.

Therefore, in handling the regulatory process that governs construction and operation stages, the company must respond not just to the grievances of residents and communities with some standing to contest their programs on the grounds of damages or inconvenience, it must also handle the sophisticated technical challenges of anti-nuclear organizations. In certain instances the opposition has attempted to block these hearings altogether.

Examples of these two approaches by the opposition to the hearing process abound. As in many other industrialized countries, the law requires public hearings at several stages of the development of a nuclear power plant. Until recently the anti-nuclear forces have relied primarily on these hearings as an opportunity to outline the technical deficiencies of the power company plans, and to warn of the possible dangers to the health and safety of the local residents.

In one recent case, the opposition tried a different approach—in a hearing sponsored by a prefectural government, demonstrators blocked the access to the auditorium where the hearing was to take place. The hearing was a critical one for the company as its request could not be approved without it. In order to comply with the regulations, the central government proposed a "long-distance" hearing, and local authorities supported this solution because they are in favor of the construction project. The company will probably agree to this approach; but it is almost certain that the legality of such a hearing will be challenged in the courts.

Organizational Change

At the outset, determining the location of nuclear plant sites, and making the necessary arrangements, was the job of the department in charge of corporate real estate in consultation with design and safety engineers. In short, the company handled nuclear plant locations in the same manner as any ordinary plant.

In the early 1970's, the company established a specialized division, chaired by a managing director, that is solely responsible for securing nuclear plant sites. This division currently employs 85 persons (53 of managerial or professional level) in five different departments. These departments include: (1) administration (eight persons concerned with legal and general questions); (2) environmental protection (thirty-nine technical specialists); (3) three departments, each specializing in development of a particular plant site, which employ thirteen, ten and fifteen individuals, respectively. This staff has its headquarters in the corporate office, but it also maintains field offices at the proposed sites.

Among those executives interviewed, the general belief was that this office had helped the company to achieve most of its objectives thus far. As one of them commented: "We believe that opposition to nuclear power is really stronger in Japan than in the United States. Still we have managed to get most of what we want because utility companies are very large in Japan (there are only nine of them), and this enables us to mobilize the technical and administrative talent that is needed to get a project through. It is a lengthy, but relatively manageable, process to negotiate with the various groups concerned. Of course, we do not negotiate with all of these people—if they are not willing to negotiate with 'sincerity' we do not talk to them at all."

CONSTRUCTION COMPANY E—The Give and Take of the Bargaining Process

Construction companies are on the cutting edge of many of the issues raised by plant location, employment and land use. To examine these issues in some detail, it is helpful to focus on some of the experiences of Construction Company E.

Since its establishment in the 1930's, the firm has cultivated a "pioneer" image. It was one of the first firms in Japan to design and build skyscrapers. It is currently involved in construction of nuclear power stations, and is among the industry leaders in overseas construction activities. Domestically, the company is engaged in the design and contruction of a broad range of residential and industrial projects. The company has substantial landholdings in several metropolitan areas, as well as many residential and office-building rental properties. These far-ranging activities have exposed Company E to pressures from local community groups, opponents of nuclear power, the government, and even, in one instance, a minority group.

Community relations is of special importance to the company. As one executive observed: "If the behavior of our employees is not up to the standard expected by the local population, if the noise from the construction site and heavy traffic of vehicles disturbs the peace, then the quality of the relationship between the firm and the residents is adversely affected. For this reason, the labor affairs and safety departments monitor each building site. These departments organize educational seminars with the staff about these sensitive community issues."

Still, some difficulties arise. Commenting on this, one executive said: "Subcontractors can be a difficult problem for us. They have a less stable labor force, which is less educated, and less inclined to follow the company's rules."

This is one of the reasons why the company attempts to hire as many local residents as it can for construction site work—particularly in rural and small-town communities. As one executive put it: "We would expect such people to be more respectful of those who live in the area. We also feel that an organized action against a project is less likely to occur if many of the jobs are filled by local residents. For the same reason, we try to rely on local subcontractors as much as we can."

To implement this policy administratively, the allocation of employment to local workers and contractors is determined in advance of the beginning of construction by joint action involving:(1) the division in charge of the project; (2) labor specialists; and (3) area managers. The share is usually expressed as a percentage of the project's total work force. Proposed wage scales are also checked against labor market conditions in the district to make sure that there are no discrepancies.

The company regards these procedures as especially important in the construction of nuclear power plants. One executive noted: "We feel that sensitivity to local subcontracting and labor helps to ease opposition to the project at the community and prefectural levels. Still it is more difficult with nuclear plant construction because it requires work of the highest quality, and that is not always available from the local labor supply. For that reason, once we have a reasonable expectation that a project will be approved, we begin a training program for prospective employees so that we will have a large pool of local workers who are at least partially qualified by the time the project is actually started."

A Japanese Minority Group

Minorities are rare in Japan—one of the most prominent examples is the burakamin. Historically, the burakamin were the lowest class of social outcasts. Individuals were stigmatized in this way because they, or their ancestors, performed jobs or services deemed "impure" by Buddhist believers. Many of these proscribed occupations were those that involved the killing of animals—for example, butchers, and tanners, and so on.

Today discrimination against burakamin is prohibited by law, but the political parties and community action groups which are most active in promoting buraku rights claim that many instances of discrimination continue. If, for example, a large-scale construction project is planned for an area near Osaka, where many burakamin live, a representative will demand that a specific share of employment and subcontracting be reserved for them. The company is as cooperative as circumstances will allow in these cases. Management feels some sense of social responsibility for the burakamin, but it also wants to avoid the violent confrontation which is advocated by some buraku groups as an option in the event that negotiations fail. For the most part, the labor unions are willing to go along with the policy toward the burakamin because the company is not proposing to hire them on a full-time basis.

Compared with the experience of other construction firms, the company feels that its relationship to the buraku groups is a good one. But management continues to be concerned, and the labor affairs department is paying close attention to the issue.

Finally, it should be noted that the success enjoyed by the burakamin with this particular company is by no means widespread. Buraku groups have also been attempting to gain access to bank employment through lawsuits and efforts to publicly embarrass the banking industry. Thus far the media—and as a result, the public—have shown little interest, and no progress has been made.

Issues in Urban Areas

While disputes as to the "proper" employment share is typical of those encountered when initiating projects in smaller communities, in more densely populated urban districts the most serious friction with residents occurs over the character and size of new projects. Most construction contracts in Japan require the general contractor to obtain the necessary permits and authorizations from local residents, even if it is building the project for another developer. In addition to the usual requirements for zoning and building permits, custom requires a visit to each house in the area near the project, and a negotiated consent to the project from each resident. To obtain the approval of residents, each branch office has a special section of full-time negotiators. In Tokyo, for example, this office has 12 persons, all of them relatively senior managers. One executive commented: "Basically, the area residents we talk to fall into one of three categories—those who will accept an offer of compensation for inconvenience caused by the project, those who want to negotiate some sort of modification in the project, and those who just will not budge."

The need for approval of local residents is, of course, not a new requirement, nor does it always raise the kinds of issues that are important to protest groups in this context—environmental, land use, and ecological questions. Still, the increasingly stubborn resistance of individuals in these circumstances owes much in technique and method—if not in substance—to the widespread proliferation and success of protest tactics.

An Executive Director of the company said: "We like to settle these cases if we can, but we also have a reputation for obtaining the necessary approval from the courts if negotiation proves unsuccessful." In Japan, rather than residents enjoining the building of a new project, the developer must go to court and obtain the "go-ahead" for its plans. For this purpose, the corporate office has established an in-house legal department that decides when the company should utilize the legal process. The company continues to rely on outside law firms for court appearances. As a general rule, the company does not go to court unless 80 to 90 percent of the residents have approved their proposal. One executive commented: "This kind of case is pretty exceptional—we do not like to do this for more than a few cases."

Senior executives are seldom involved in these types of negotiations, but there have even been exceptions to that rule. When the company built a high-rise residential tower in a Tokyo suburb, where the average building was only two floors high, the Executive Vice President spent over one month negotiating approval of the construction with local government and political leadership and with community activists. The project was eventually approved after the company incorporated some facilities for community use in a modified plan.

Whenever possible, the company seeks consensus. In a recent case, the company development plan for a residential area near a major city called for the construction of a large supermarket serving the needs of old and new residents. In response, the local retailers' association opposed the plan because they felt threatened by the competition. In an example of how protest techniques are sometimes appropriated to serve conventional economic interests, they organized a protest demonstration in front of the company's headquarters. This action attracted the attention of the press and television networks that condemned the company for its "selfish behavior."

The company's response was to suspend construction of the supermarket and to delegate a general manager to negotiate outstanding issues with representatives of the retailers' association in the hope that an agreement could be reached which would protect the merchants from adverse economic impact. The company was successful in achieving this objective and executives interviewed said: "It was our willingness to negotiate with sincerity, rather than any specific points of settlement, that was decisive." Once again, the importance of "sincerity" was emphasized—another reminder that in Japan both the style and the substance of discussions are vital.

In line with this view, the company feels that its image has an important impact on how it can handle delicate negotiations. One executive said: "I think that our positive image helps us to present our side of the story to the public. Public opinion in Japan is increasingly critical of 'big business,' which is blamed for rising prices in land and housing."

STEEL COMPANY F—Plant Closure in the Land of "Lifetime Employment"

Much has been written about Japan's system of "lifetime employment" or, as one executive describes it, "lifetime employment until retirement," and its contribution to labor stability and harmony. The experience of Steel Company F shows that the concept of "lifetime employment" is, in reality, a far from certain or universal proposition. In spite of this less than total commitment to "lifetime employment" in practice, its ideal lives on in the minds of plant workers and the communities in which they reside. These factors make a plant closure in times of a contracting economy an especially painful process for a Japanese company. Still, however difficult such closures may be to manage in the Japanese environment, they do occur, and the experience of Steel Company F is a case in point.

Since the 1973 oil crisis, and the subsequent slowdown of Japanese industry from what had been double-digit growth, the country's steel industry has suffered from overcapacity and high operating costs. One of the strategies developed to overcome the effects of sluggish demand was "rationalization"—a substantial streamlining of production through the closing of unprofitable segments of the production process and the elimination of surplus jobs. Steel was not alone in its rationalization efforts—many other industries such as aluminum, synthetic fibers, and shipbuilding were also involved in this process.

In 1978, the company's plants were operating at 70 percent of their capacity. As a result, the board of directors authorized the corporate planning office's recommendation to close some facilities—particularly the largely underutilized rolling mills. The plan recommended the closing of several facilities, taking care that these closings were spread around the country. It was assumed that no regular full-time, permanent employee would be dismissed as a result of production cutbacks.

One of the large installations that the company decided

to close was in a region with relatively little industry. In 1978, the company employed several thousand regular full-time workers at various locations within the region. In addition, the company provided jobs for nearly as many additional persons either by subcontracting or through the need for occasional part-time work. In addition, many enterprises had over 50 percent of their business tied to the company's operations.

Company F is one of the largest steel manufacturers in Japan, and the production at the steel works in this area accounted for only 3 percent of its total capacity in Japan. From the local perspective, however, the plant was crucial to the community. The installation's share of the total manufacturing production in the city was 78.5 percent the year before the proposed closings, and the share of prefectural manufacturing was over 15 percent. This plant's share would be reduced by over 30 percent if one of its facilities was closed down. Furthermore, tax payments to local governments would be affected—the company provided 36.5 percent of all tax revenues for the city, and 2.5 percent of prefectural revenue. A decline in shipments would affect the taxes assessed, particularly at the city level. Of course, the reduced earnings of local residents would also affect the city and prefectural tax base.

The importance of these steelworks was far larger than in any other location where F plants were located. This was due in large measure to the fact that the prefecture where these plants were established is one of Japan's underdeveloped regions with few opportunities for alternative employment for those who lost their jobs as a result of the closing. In addition, some time prior to 1978 another large local employer, an iron-ore mining company, announced that it would close its only mine in the area by early 1980 and lay off 700 employees. By the time the steel company said it would close its mill, the community was not willing to accept this decision without resistance.

Although the company anticipated an unfavorable reaction to its announcement of a plant closure, it did not expect a strong and coordinated opposition. It told the union that none of its workers then employed at the affected facility would be discharged, that the reduction of the labor force would be achieved by natural attrition and transfers to other installations at the company's expense. The company also told union officials that it had no intention of further reducing activity—its intentions were limited to this particular mill.

In spite of these assurances, the union leaders were skeptical. They believed that the economic viability of the various other local operations of the company were tied to the facility that the company wanted to close. As a result, the company union, which represented all full-time, nonmanagerial employees, was willing to join forces with the local labor federation that represented many of the unions of employees of subcontracting

firms. Other groups also got involved—an anti-closing resolution was passed by the City Council, and the mayor mobilized the local Diet representatives to put pressure on the company.

The opposition utilized various strategies. A demonstration was organized in front of the steel works in which a large number of union members and local residents participated. City Hall even paid for anti-company posters that urged opposition to the decision. One sign erected in front of the main railroad station said: "Let us mobilize the power of all citizens to make Company F withdraw its business-rationalization program." The mayor also supervised a petition drive which obtained the signatures of 40,000 of the city's 70,000 residents. This petition was presented to the president of the company amidst much fanfare and publicity.

Meanwhile, the Diet representatives had not been idle. They demanded help from the Prime Minister, the Ministry of Trade, and the Finance Ministry in averting the shutdown. City officials charged that the company had "betrayed" them. They cited a harbor expansion which the company had recently requested and which was granted over the opposition of local fishermen because of the company's then substantial participation in the local economy. Under these circumstances, even the Prime Minister said that "he would do all he could to find the solution to the probable job losses."

The issue received widespread media coverage, at both local and national levels. The company's file of clippings on the episode was more than two inches thick, and many news items related to the incident were carried on different television stations. The vehemence of the opposition surprised the company. One executive, who was involved from the beginning recalled: "The company was a bit slow to respond. Even after we sensed the need, it took time to put together the data on the ties of the steel works to the local economy, and the full impact of the shutdown.

Once it had compiled the necessary data, the company pursued a two-tiered negotiating strategy. On one level, the President and the Executive Vice President of Corporate Planning began to meet with Diet members, high officials of the national government, the prefectural governor, and the mayor for ceremonial exchanges. As one of the executives put it: "We thought it was important to demonstrate sincerity in our willingness to accommodate the wishes of local residents to the extent possible, given the economic imperatives."

On another level, a team of managers from the corporate planning staff and the labor relations section began negotiating with the unions. The key element in this strategy was the company union. It was felt that without its support it would be almost impossible to get the community leaders to drop their objections. During these substantive negotiations the company argued that if the shutdown were not implemented quickly, the low operating ratio would generate more substantial losses and more drastic measures might be necessary.

In contrast to the dire picture the company painted of the consequences of prolonged delay, it also emphasized the advantages of going ahead with its plans, company executives reaffirmed a pledge not to lay off any permanent employees and to minimize cutbacks among subcontractors. (Provided, of course, that its "rationalization" plan went ahead and no further losses were incurred.)

Looking to the future, the company promised a detailed plan which would articulate its "vision" as to the plant's operation and how jobs in the area could best be preserved. After four months of negotiations, the major company union voiced tentative approval. Armed with this tacit union backing, the company negotiated with representatives of the city. In these talks the company argued that time was of the essence—the "rationalization" plan must be implemented immediately before losses mounted to the point where the very existence of all local operations would be in jeopardy. It was also argued that this approach was the most sensible in terms of preserving the city's tax base: By shutting down the unprofitable segment, it would actually make more money. In the event that this calculation proved to be inaccurate, the company promised to cooperate with the city in finding ways to reduce the adverse impact of the lower revenues. After several more months of intensive negotiations, Company F had succeeded in neutralizing enough of the opposition to proceed with the shutdown after what amounted to a minor delay.

Looking back on the experience, the executive director in charge of the negotiations felt that three major strategies had contributed to success:

"First, it was the affirmation of the no lay-off policy that finally swayed the leadership of the company union. To convince these people, we had to back that pledge up with substantive assurances—we negotiated a 'loan' of our employees to those companies, many of them in other areas, that urgently needed skilled personnel. Under this arrangement, the transferred worker received regular pay from the 'new' employer, while our company paid for any difference in salary and costs of relocation.

"Secondly, we had to demonstrate our willingness to keep the rest of the local operations open, even if it might have been cheaper in the long run to write off the entire operation. This promise was also a useful bargaining tool in negotiations.

"Finally, I think that our tradition of good relations with the community ultimately paid off. Although there was initial hostility, in the long run our 'vision' of the future was accepted at face value because we were trusted, and we did reach an agreement."

Although company officials thought the opposition, and the need for cooperation, had been underestimated, the episode brought little in the way of lasting organizational change. As one executive stated: "We need to know more about the impact of these kinds of decisions on the local economy and we have to incorporate this knowledge into our planning. From now on, the corporate planning division will collect these data in cooperation with plant managers at the plant in question. We also need better communications with unions. We have not made any explicit organizational changes because that would formally acknowledge that the company is seriously considering other plant closures. Obviously we do not want to do that."

THE TRADING COMPANY—Public Opinion and Public Accountability

Japanese trading companies, "sogo shosha," are primarily intermediaries—acting as a link between producers and consumers, primarily in the manufacturing sector. As such, they have seldom been a target of outside pressure from environmentalists, consumer advocates, or community activists. The size and scope of their operations, however, make their activities naturally suspect to the media and the general public.

These suspicions are not of entirely recent origin. Traditionally, merchants were not greatly respected in Japanese society. In postwar Japan, the trading companies succeeded in developing a "transformed" image—largely through the confluence of favorable circumstances. This "transformation" was the result of Japan's yearning for a respected world position in which the trading companies were among the country's most visible international representatives. The media promoted the figure of the "shosha man," diligently selling Japanese goods abroad under the most challenging circumstances and stimulating economic growth at home in the process. This highly favorable public acceptance continued even after the "growth at all cost" policy was widely criticized in the wake of air and water pollution incidents that adversely affected manufacturing companies.

With the abolition of fixed exchange rates in 1971, the honeymoon with the media was over. Many trading companies began to speculate against the dollar. Although this activity was immensely profitable, much of the goodwill evaporated as a result of unforeseen consequences of currency speculation.

The speculation strategy called for massive dollar loans to be repaid in the future with revalued yen. As the companies had no use for the additional credit in their regular business operations, they began to invest in certain commodities and real estate. This massive involvement increased demand pressure on already overheated markets and the price of many necessities, as well as housing and land, skyrocketed. The public was angry and the media began to blame trading company speculation for shortages and price hikes.

The trading companies never recovered their pre-1971 prestige. To make matters worse, various incidents involving illegal activities of executives and managers (notably the Lockheed scandal) made the public increasingly suspicious of the motives of trading companies under any circumstances.

The Spot Market Incident

At the present, the handling of outside pressure by trading companies is still predominantly reactive in nature. A case in point is the campaign in defense of purchases of oil on the spot market. The press charged that the purchase by trading companies of oil on the spot market has contributed to the upward pressure on oil prices. Some of the companies have been accused of shipping oil purchased under long-term contract to Europe, while the more expensive spot-market oil was supplied to Japan.

In responding to these charges the manager of one company, who has responsibility for buying oil, met with the press and attacked the errors in the news stories. Not content with the coverage afforded by the "press club," the department also initiated a "study group" on the problems of the world oil trade. This, of course, gave the company the prerogative of selecting various influential personalities to exchange ideas and information on the subject. In the process, the necessity of inviting an entire "press club" was avoided. The campaign was considered a success, though many managers are unhappy with the levels of expertise of most of the journalists. Commenting on this problem, one executive said: "They rotate these people fairly rapidly from one assignment to another, and they have little or no time to develop the knowledge required to understand the issues thoroughly."

This difficulty is not limited to the press, it is also encountered when dealing with the government. As one manager noted: "I think that a lot of the problems that we have had with the Ministry of Trade could have been avoided, if they would just let these officials get some experience in one place. But they move them to another position before that is possible."

Company Organization

Systematic daily contact with reporters is a fairly new enterprise for trading companies. One of the companies interviewed only established its public relations section in 1974. This section is part of the corporate planning division and is currently staffed by sixteen employees, one of whom is the general manager. In addition to relations with the media, this office coordinates the assembling of information on subjects of public interest within the company, and supervises in-house publications and business-related advertisements. Decision making, however, is concentrated in relatively few hands—"political" public relations is controlled by the public relations general manager and one other employee of managerial rank. These proposals are then approved by the executive vice president for administration, who will bring in other top executives—including the president or chairman—when they are needed. (This is done regularly for biannual press conferences.) Clearly the Japanese style of decision making, "ringi," is rarely used in managing the company's public relations. Unlike most activities in the Japanese business environment, most of these actions are reactive and require a rapid response. As a result, decisions are taken after brief consultations between the public relations general manager, the executive vice president for administration, and the manager in charge of the product area involved.

Although company executives feel that the organization has responded effectively to media criticism, some think that the approach has been too defensive. They would like to see their company take more initiative in its relations with the public. Some mentioned a Mobil-type of advertising campaign but, at the present time, the company is not willing to provide the financial support for this kind of activity. The company does buy half-page ads in a major business daily, but their value is doubtful, in the view of some managers, as the readers are pro-business in the first place. A major emphasis in the future will be on internal public relations. One executive put it this way: "I think that we get our point across best when our own employees, who, after all, are their friends and neighbors, explain our position to the public. This can be a lot more effective than advertisements or press conferences."

DEALING WITH THE PUBLIC—A Tale of Two Companies

The experiences of a food company and a cosmetics company reveal a great deal as to what it takes to earn the approval of consumer groups as a "socially responsible" organization. By American or European standards both of these companies would be considered responsible and responsive organizations. One of them, however, enjoys better relations with consumer organizations than the other.

The key to this greater public acceptance, as it so often is in Japanese society, may be found in differing approaches—one company emphasizes "maximum consultation" and assumes the "sincerity" of many of its critics, while the other company focuses on the delivery of information to the public and avoids direct contact with consumer organizations.

On balance, it would appear from these examples that

there is no substitute for active dialogue with pressure groups in Japanese society. The willingness to engage in these kinds of confrontations in a calm and reasonable manner is seen by both business and pressure groups as a real test of "sincerity."

"Sincerity," as all of these case studies have amply illustrated, is the real threshold of accommodation. While many different examples and definitions of this concept emerge, the common denominator in all of these discussions is that "sincerity" comes from the firm conviction that the essential rightness of one's position can be proven to the satisfaction of a reasonable person. One who possesses this kind of assurance is, as a result, willing to discuss a sensible accommodation with other "sincere" individuals. These discussions have at least the appearance of meetings on a basis of equality, because the test for access is supposed to be "sincerity" rather than the ability to inflict harm.

There is evidence that even the most militant consumer activists appreciate the fine distinction between a company whose apparent motive is fear and one that is moved by "sincerity." One of Japan's leading consumer advocates commented on this difference: "Once we have done our research, we try to discuss the issues directly with the company. We often find that the chief of the consumer section, who is usually our initial contact, is afraid, but not sincere." It is, therefore, on the fine distinction between fear and sincerity that much of the success of Japanese public relations may depend.

A Food Company

A food company, an organization which wins a high level of approval from consumer organizations, is one of the oldest Japanese manufacturers of food additives, processed foods, and cooking oils. Its product mix consists of additives and seasonings, cooking oils, vegetable proteins, processed foods (mainly products licensed from overseas), and specialty chemicals for pharmaceutical purposes. Besides its operations in Japan, the company has seven overseas manufacturing facilities and numerous sales offices. Well over 10,000 persons are employed in its domestic and international operations.

One of the company's key product lines is food additives. Company executives feel especially vulnerable as food additives are increasingly becoming a target for consumer activists. In fact, the company's key product line until recently has had an MSG base. In the early 1970's, monosodium glutamate was investigated by the U.S. Food and Drug Administration (FDA). Reflecting on that period, one executive commented: "I think that an unfavorable ruling in the United States would have been adopted by the Japanese government. Fortunately for us, the opinion was favorable. This helped us to recognize the importance of better 'two-way' com-

munications with consumer groups. We were particularly concerned at that point about the public confusion between different kinds of additives. MSG, a glutamate, was often thought to be a cyclamate, which was banned by the FDA."

The company's response to the growing concern over additives was to diversify its product lines (processed foods recently became the principal sales item), to implement a communications program targeted to consumers, and to increase cooperation with independent research laboratories around the world (particularly in the United States) in order to obtain advance information about potential health hazards.

The director of the company's public relations department explained this "two-way" system of communication: "The aim of the 'two-way' communications program is to establish a *permanent* dialogue with consumers. This is in contrast to the 'one-way' advertising in the mass media. We emphasize face-to-face exchanges between consumers and company personnel.

"For this purpose we held over 1,500 meetings last year (each session involved approximately 50 participants) in which various topics relating to company products were discussed. In these meetings we try to focus on consumer experience with our products and on their complaints and suggestions for improvement. We avoid sales advertising and introduction of new products. If problems do emerge during the discussion, the appropriate department in charge of a particular product is informed directly and asked for a response."

The company has several sections that deal with the public. The public relations department is independent from sales promotion, which is responsible for advertising, and it directs "official" relations with the media and with free-lance journalists. In addition, the department publishes four newsletters for different segments of the public: (1) housewives, (2) wholesalers, (3) researchers, and (4) "opinion leaders." The first two newsletters appear on a monthly basis; the others are biannual publications. Distribution is by direct mail, but the housewives' publication also utilizes additional channels.

In addition to the public relations department, the company has a consumer bureau, which also has four sections with different responsibilities. One section maintains contacts with organized consumer groups and with grass-roots activists around the country; the second section handles claims and complaints addressed to the company; the third group organizes "Cooking Plazas," where meetings with consumers are scheduled; and the fourth office is responsible for the company's cooking schools. The consumer bureau has a staff of sixty—half of them located in the main office and the rest in seven of the local branches.

Top executives are also involved in various communications programs. As the current president has considerable experience in public relations, he does participate in discussions with outsiders. The main line of responsibility, however, lies with the Executive Vice President for Administration. He meets with consumer groups in the corporate office and represents the company at various conferences sponsored by consumer organizations or agencies of local government. One such conference was recently held in Kobe and the Executive Vice President was one of the lecturers.

In another aspect of its consumer relations program, the board of directors sponsored a lecture on food-product safety given by the former head of the U.S. Food and Drug Administration. Among lower ranking personnel, heads of the Consumer Bureau and the Public Relations department are active members of the Consumer Affairs Professionals in Business, a recently established organization of managers who are responsible for consumer affairs in their respective firms.

Commenting on reasons for his organization's success in its relations with consumers, one executive said: "I think that consumers have a good opinion of us because they accept 'the sincerity' of our commitment to a dialogue with them. This 'sincerity' has certainly been put to the test—some of the criticism is rather stiff. We are especially interested in exchanges with organized consumer groups. Our 'open door' policy encourages communication with them and we are careful to separate this activity from traditional sales promotion. We also actively solicit suggestions to improve our products—particularly in the areas of nutrition and health."

Evidently, the company's approach has been a success. Several consumer groups gave it high marks for socially responsible attitudes and openness to dialogue with consumers.

A Cosmetics Company

Although this company pursues a similar "two-way communication" approach in its relations with the public, it has been less successful than the food company in impressing consumer organizations with its "sincerity." This is due in part to the differences between the companies with respect to size and industry—but it is also relevant that the less successful program does not actively engage its opposition in any sort of meaningful debate or dialogue.

The company's position as one of Japan's largest cosmetics manufacturers puts it on the front lines as one of the consumer movement's major offensives. Consumer groups have made the safety and deceptive advertising of cosmetics a major issue with the rallying cry for their campaign: the slogans "No makeup is the best makeup," and "Cosmetics are basically alien to your skin."

Commenting bluntly on the role of size in the target-selection process, one consumer advocate said: "Our strategy is to try to expose the practices of a highly visible company. After that, the others fall into line." Another leader notes why this cosmetics firm was a particularly good choice for attack: "We are better off hitting them on specific points and scaring the others, rather than spreading our efforts too thinly across the whole industry. We also think that the leading firms are more concerned about maintaining an 'image' which is necessary to keep their edge over competitors, and thus they are more vulnerable to outside criticism."

A recent charge is that the company markets many of its products without adequate clinical testing. Currently, every new cosmetic must be authorized by the Health Ministry, but the requirements, in the opinion of consumer activists, are not sufficient to protect the public from potential health hazards. For this reason, consumer groups have launched a campaign for a change in regulations that would require the cosmetics industry to furnish the public with the same kind of data currently provided by drug manufacturers. To illustrate the need for new regulation, consumer groups have sued the company on behalf of "victims' groups," whose members claim to have incurred skin injuries after using the company's products.

One of the company's major initiatives in responding to these and other charges, is its "conflict prevention" program. Dealers are encouraged to refer any potential problems immediately to the company's field offices. Where only minor allergies are involved, the company will give the customer free cosmetics (without investigating the merits of their claims). If there are more severe difficulties, the customer is referred to a physician, with the company paying the bill for treatment regardless of whether its products are proven to be at fault. Information on these incidents is collected by the corporate office and appropriate departments are informed of any significant trend in customer complaints.

In addition to the prompt disposition of customer claims, the company also emphasizes "customer education," because management feels that most problems are caused by the inappropriate use of their products. Training programs are organized by sales branches and by some large dealers—many of which are department stores. The firm also has a counseling center in the corporate office which answers mail, telephone and "walk-in" questions. In coordination with the public relations department, the counseling center issues publications which answer the most frequently asked questions, and describe the appropriate use of various cosmetic products. These booklets are also distributed through dealership and sales outlet networks. Another technique that is used to enhance the company's image is the invitation to the public to visit its laboratories and production facilities.

This firm also publishes specialized newsletters. In addition to the press releases for the media, a quarterly bulletin is mailed to physicians who specialize in skin care, and there is a monthly newsletter for the benefit of banks, major businesses, and the rest of the cosmetics industry. The company also publishes a bulletin for lawyers whose field of expertise is consumer claims and complaints. Internal publications also deal with consumer-related issues. As one executive put it: "The principal aim of all this activity is to prevent a conflict with customers from developing to the point where it damages our credibility with the public." Asked why the company had thus far avoided direct dealings with those consumer groups that are most critical of its products, one manager said: "We do not think that they are interested in an objective discussion."

Although the company's commitment to its "conflict prevention" program continues, managers are confident that their position would be vindicated in any legal battle. As one of them expressed it: "It is difficult to establish a causal link between the use of cosmetics products and a particular skin injury." "Yet," this individual added, "insurance companies are so afraid of unsubstantiated claims that they refuse to issue product liability insurance on most lines of cosmetics."

Unlike the food company, the cosmetics company's top executives are seldom involved in any aspect of its consumer relations program. Within the public relations department 50 employees, 25 with managerial rank, deal with consumer affairs. This staff of fifty is divided into four sections (public relations, and three consumer sections with particular territories). The Tokyo area section also coordinates nationwide activities.

External Forces and Decision Making in Japan: An Assessment

Any discussion of the role of external forces in the Japanese business environment must begin with an important caveat. Japan is a land of contradiction and paradox. While some of these inconsistencies can be reconciled, not all of them can be explained.

In the business world, for example, the country is the envy of all its competitors for its industrial harmony and apparent commitment to growth and expansion. Yet the Minemata chemical and Narita airport episodes, to name only two of the more prominent examples, were conflicts of unusual ferocity by any standards. Both of these cases resulted in sabotage, injury—and at least a few examples of hand-to-hand combat between the protagonists. No effort will be made here to explain the conflict between the placid image of the textbook and the occasional violence of reality, except to say that neither impression is a wholly accurate depiction of the way things work.

To understand, therefore, how business institutions handle the intrusion of external forces into the decision-making process it is necessary to focus on more modest objectives than the reconciling of extraordinarily contradictory modes of social behavior. Consistent with the view that conflict rarely arises in Japanese society, one observer noted that there is a stoic acceptance of many existing conditions, even among influential consumer advocates, that would be a subject of protest in other countries. He said: "The most interesting cases are those that do not come up. I was talking to a leading consumer advocate, the 'Esther Peterson of Japan,' and I asked her to explain the reason for the high rate of inflation in Japanese food costs. She said to me, 'So-ne' which translates, that's the way it is."

It is, of course, impossible to study "cases that do not arise," but a look at the ones that have (repeatedly in one form or another) reveals something about those issues that are considered legitimate subjects of protest and those which are not.

To begin with, there is little apparent concern with abstract concepts of equity in Japan. The emphasis is more practical—or reciprocal—a fair exchange of privileges and responsibilities in a given situation. The accusation that a company is "unfair" to its workers, shareholders or local residents is a rare one, and not capable of enlisting great sympathy. To that extent, the popular image of stoic resignation to the vicissitudes of fate has some validity.

Secondly, there is no widespread belief in any sort of "inherent rights." The notion that individuals have "rights" is infrequently invoked, despite the fact that the Japanese Constitution, written during the American occupation, grants "rights"—particularly to women. In spite of this, feminism is not a particularly strong movement in Japan, and feminists would have little success in relying on constitutional prescriptions to enlist support.

There is, however, one overriding principle in Japanese life that governs relations between persons and institutions, and that is the importance of "responsibility" which is based on respect for these reciprocal exchanges of privileges and obligations. As a result of these mutually binding relationships, an individual has a responsibility to his company to act in the best interests of the organization he serves, and a business has responsibility to society to act in harmony with society's interests.

To disturb this complex network of reciprocal relationships can seriously damage a company's credibility with the public and with the government. For this reason such industrial derelictions as air and water pollution and hazardous products can arouse great indignation. These kinds of public behavior are not accepted with stoic resignation. There are also historical reasons—one of them fairly recent, the other long-standing—which account for the reluctance of business to disturb this fragile equilibrium. Most recent, and often cited, is the scarcity of resources. Actually this is a fairly new problem for Japan. Until the early part of this century Japan's population density was less than that of most European countries. Still, the explosive growth in the last half-century has created a sense of urgency about this problem that is an important factor in Japanese political life. The second force which creates a powerful pull toward accommodation is the *memory of chaos*.

Although it has been over three centuries since the Togukawa Shogunate put an end to a period of lawlessness and anarchy, the awareness of what a horrible period this was, and the fragile base on which order rests, is kept alive in the minds of the Japanese citizenry—from school child to company president. In contrast to the United States, where the vast abundance and national consensus once made it possible for a business leader to say—if, in fact—he did: "What's good for General Motors is good for the country," the working hypothesis in Japan may well be the reverse. There is so little of everything to go around in Japan and consensus as to objectives is so tenuous that it is often necessary to determine in advance, through consultation with various groups, whether what is good for Company A is good for Japan.

It is from this central fact that the Japanese system of conflict management—"maximum consultation"—has evolved. For reasons of economy and efficiency, as well as social custom, companies rarely deal with individual grievants. In any event, the foundation of social order which is the precondition of business success rests on the successful accommodation of groups, not individuals. For this reason, the views of a legitimately constituted group, whether local property owners or "victims'" organizations, must be listened to, accorded weight, and even accommodated, often in circumstances where the relative balance of power does not require compromise.

Because custom commands that this ongoing negotiating process be part of the fabric of commercial life, it is vitally important that a company project the image of trust, reliability and integrity that will earn the respect, if not the acquiescence, of its negotiating partners. For this reason a company's image is important in its own right. It is not merely helpful that an organization create a positive public impression, it is critical to the successful conduct of its business affairs.

The central position of negotiation in the framework of conflict adjustment results in a subordinate and relatively unimportant role for the rule of law. The legal process cannot resolve a dispute because it is necessary not to defeat an adversary but to get the opponent to accept a point of view and to cooperate once an accommodation has been reached. A courtroom defeat by resort to abstract concepts (which are not really believed in with great conviction anyway) accomplishes nothing. The wounded adversary will continue to be troublesome—what is needed is a compromise that both parties can live with. Furthermore, it is necessary to use this conflict constructively to establish a continuing dialogue so that problems of this kind are avoided.

This refusal to agree to the supremacy of law—which is the final arbiter of disputes in many countries—means that Japanese companies will only acknowledge responsibility when it can be proven in a personal sense, and without resort to legal abstractions. Thus, if a company's actions can be proven to have been the proximate cause of an injury, Japanese companies are usually receptive to a settlement. Where, however, the company is asked to accept strict liability on the ground that certain activities or products are inherently dangerous, and there is no proof of fault, they are unusually resistant. Because responsibility is such a serious matter to them, and it goes to the root of their perceived effectiveness, they are not willing to assume it simply as a cost of doing business.

This report has focused on the day-to-day activities of a representative number of Japanese companies. For this reason, many of the most notorious cases—such as the early Minemata pollution incident, the Narita airport controversy, and the struggle for prefectural bans on synthetic detergents—have been mentioned, if at all, only in passing. The emphasis has been on the ordinary daily conduct of business. These interviews show a society in which conflict is no stranger, and where the methods of resolution are eccentric by many standards but, nevertheless, effective.

Related Conference Board Publications